PUBLISHER COMMENTARY

There is a reason the U.S. Air Force has one of the best cyberwarfare weapon system programs.

This book pulls together 4 key Air Force publications on Cyberspace Operations.

AFPD 17-2	CYBERSPACE OPERATIONS	12 Apr 2016
AFI 10-1701	COMMAND AND CONTROL (C2) FOR CYBERSPACE OPERATIONS	5 Mar 2014
AFI 33-200	AIR FORCE CYBERSECURITY PROGRAM MANAGEMENT	16 Feb 2016
AFI 33-150	MANAGEMENT OF CYBERSPACE SUPPORT ACTIVITIES	30 Nov 2011

These publications cover guidelines for planning and conducting cyberspace operations to support the warfighter and achieve national security objectives. AFPD 17-2 and the Unified Command Plan in AFI 10-1701 provides guidance required to operate and defend the DoDIN and direct other cyberspace operations. AFI 33-200 establishes the Air Force Cybersecurity program and risk management framework as an essential element to accomplishing the mission. AFI 33-150 provides guidance intended to assist Air Force personnel in identifying activities required to support Air Force communications. The Air Force Policy Directive (AFPD) and the Air Force Instructions (AFI), developed in conjunction with other governing directives, prescribe procedures for Air Force Cyberspace Operations and Program Management. They AFPD 17-2 applies to all Air Force information systems (ISs), and information technology (IT) infrastructure. It also assigns certain roles and responsibilities to the Air Force Office of Special Investigations (AFOSI) and discusses the Cybersecurity Strategies in detail.

The instruction is an initiative to reduce the number of SAF/CIO A6 departmental- level publications by changing their publications from "stove-piped" system/program-based to audience/role-based focus. Topics covered include logistics support and life-cycle management plans, engineering and installation governance, IT acquisition support, project and program implementation services, and requirements review, preparation, and processing.

Why buy a book you can download for free? We print this so you don't have to.

Some documents are only distributed in <u>electronic media</u>. Some online docs are missing some pages or the graphics are barely legible. When a new standard is released, an engineer prints it out, punches holes and puts it in a 3-ring binder. While this is not a big deal for a 5 or 10-page document, many cyber documents are over 100 pages and printing a large document is a time-consuming effort. So, an engineer that's paid $75 an hour is spending hours simply printing out the tools needed to do the job. That's time that could be better spent doing engineering. We publish these documents so engineers can focus on what they were hired to do – engineering.

A list of **Cybersecurity Standards** we publish is attached at the end of this document.

BY ORDER OF THE SECRETARY
OF THE AIR FORCE

AIR FORCE POLICY DIRECTIVE 17-2

12 APRIL 2016

Cyberspace

CYBERSPACE OPERATIONS

COMPLIANCE WITH THIS PUBLICATION IS MANDATORY

OPR: AF/A3CO-A6CO

Certified by: SAF/CIO A6
(Lt Gen Bender)

Supersedes: AFPD 10-17, 31 July 2012;
AFPD 33-1, 9 August 2012

Pages: 11

This Air Force (AF) Policy Directive (PD) (AFPD) consolidates cyberspace operations policy previously included in superseded AFPDs and implements: Presidential Policy Directive-20, *U.S. Cyber Operations Policy*; Department of Defense (DoD) Directive (DoDD) 3222.03, *DoD Electromagnetic Environmental Effects (E3) Program*; DoDD 3700.01, *DoD Command and Control (C2) Enabling Capabilities*; DoDD 3710.01, *National Leadership Command Capability (NLCC)*, DoDD 8000.01, *Management of the Department of Defense Information Enterprise*; DoDD 8100.02, *Use of Commercial Wireless Devices, Services, and Technologies in the Department of Defense Global Information Grid (GIG)*; DoDD O-8530.1, *Computer Network Defense*; DoD Instruction (DoDI) O-3710.02, *Secretary of Defense Communications (SDC)*; DoDI 4630.09, *Communications Waveform Development and Standardization*; DoDI 4650.01, *Policy and Procedures for Management and Use of the Electromagnetic Spectrum;* DoDI 4650.02, *Military Auxiliary Radio System (MARS)*; DoDI 5000.02, Operation of the Defense Acquisition System, DoDI 8100.04, *DoD Unified Capabilities (UC)*; DoDI 8140.01, *Cyberspace Workforce Management*; DoDI 8320.02, *Sharing Data, Information, and Information Technology (IT) Services in the Department of Defense;* DoDI 8410.01, *Internet Domain Name Use and Approval;* DoDI 8410.02, *NetOps for the Global Information Grid (GIG)*; DoDI 8410.03, *Network Management*; DoDI 8420.01, *Commercial Wireless Local-Area Network (WLAN) Devices, Systems, and Technologies;* DoDI 8500.01, *Cybersecurity;* DoDI 8520.02, *Public Key Infrastructure (PKI) and Public Key (PK) Enabling;* DoDI 8520.03, *Identity Authentication for Information Systems;* DoDI 8523.01, *Communications Security (COMSEC);* DoDI O-8530.2, *Support to Computer Network Defense (CND)*; and, CJCSI 3121.01B, *Standing Rules of Engagement/Standing Rules for the Use of Force for US Forces.*

SUMMARY OF CHANGES

This AFPD, published along with AFPD 17-1, supersedes AFPDs 10-17, 33-1, and portions of AFPD 33-5. It aligns and consolidates policies on cyberspace operations with current AF doctrine, statutory, and regulatory guidelines.

This AFPD provides policy guidelines for planning and conducting AF cyberspace operations to support the warfighter and achieve national security objectives. It applies to all information, information systems (ISs), and information technology (IT) infrastructure within Air Force purview, excluding non-Air Force space, Special Access Programs (SAP), and Intelligence Community ISs. Non-Air Force space systems are multi-Component space systems (e.g., those supporting more than one DoD Component) and are under the purview of United States Strategic Command. It applies to all military and civilian AF personnel, members of the AF Reserve, Air National Guard, and individuals or organizations authorized by an appropriate government official to conduct cyberspace operations or to access the AF Information Network (AFIN). Ensure that all records created as a result of processes prescribed in this publication are maintained in accordance with AF Manual (AFMAN) 33-363, *Management of Records*, and disposed of in accordance with the Air Force Records Disposition Schedule (RDS) located in the AF Records Information Management System (AFRIMS). Refer recommended changes and questions about this publication to the office of primary responsibility (OPR) using AF Form 847, *Recommendation for Change of Publication*; route AF Forms 847 from the field through the submitting organization's chain of command.

1. Overview. This Directive establishes AF policy for planning and executing operations to achieve Information Dominance in cyberspace.

2. Policy. It is AF policy that:

2.1. The AF will achieve Information Dominance by fully exploiting the man-made domain of cyberspace to execute, enhance and support Air Force core missions.

2.2. The AF will execute Cyberspace Operations to support joint warfighter requirements, increase effectiveness of its core missions, increase resiliency, survivability, and cybersecurity of its information and systems, and realize efficiencies through innovative IT solutions.

2.2.1. Successful execution of Cyberspace Operations requires integrated and synchronized execution of Offensive Cyberspace Operations (OCO), Defensive Cyberspace Operations (DCO), and DoD Information Networks (DoDIN) Operations (DoDIN Ops) as described in Joint Publication (JP) 3-12, *Cyberspace Operations*.

2.2.2. The AF will develop cyberspace weapon systems; capabilities; operational tactics, techniques, and procedures (TTPs); and maintenance procedures to execute AF and Joint cyberspace operations.

2.2.3. AF Cyberspace Operations will be conducted by Airmen trained and certified in accordance with applicable DoD, Joint, and Intelligence Community directives and authorities.

2.2.4. The AF will develop weapons systems, capabilities, and TTPs to "fight through" enemy offensive cyberspace operations to ensure continued mission assurance in hostile cyber environments.

2.3. AFIN Operations are actions taken to design, build, configure, secure, operate, maintain, and sustain AF IT, to include Platform IT (PIT), cyber enabled systems/weapons systems, and National Security Systems (NSS), in a way that creates and preserves data availability, integrity and confidentiality.

2.4. AFIN Operations will be planned and conducted to ensure enhanced information sharing, collaboration, and situational awareness within the Joint Information Environment.

2.5. Data, information, and IT services will be made visible, accessible, understandable, trusted, and interoperable throughout their lifecycles for all authorized users.

2.6. The AF will centrally command, control, and manage the AFIN infrastructure and enterprise services.

3. **Responsibilities.**

3.1. Deputy Chief of Staff for Intelligence, Surveillance, and Reconnaissance (ISR) (AF/A2) will:

3.1.1. Oversee development of specialized ISR capabilities, resources, products, and services to support cyberspace operational requirements.

3.1.2. Ensure development of ISR TTPs to enable cyberspace operations.

3.1.3. Develop policy and provide guidance and oversight for Cyberspace ISR.

3.2. Deputy Chief of Staff, Operations (AF/A3) will:

3.2.1. Develop policy and provide guidance and oversight for OCO, DCO Response Actions, DCO Internal Defensive Measures, and C2 of cyberspace operations, integrating the activities of the AF's operations, ISR, and cyberspace communities to ensure the delivery of cyberspace operational capabilities to warfighters. Cyberspace operational capabilities include, but are not limited to, the deployment and employment of cyber weapon systems, non-kinetic operations, cyber-electronic warfare support, cyber ISR, combatant commander-directed/prioritized operational planning, cyber mission force (CMF) operations, and cyber operations conducted by other than CMFs (e.g., counterintelligence operations conducted by the AF Office of Special Investigations (AFOSI)).

3.2.2. Have primary responsibility for oversight of AF cyberspace operations, except for activities assigned or reserved to SAF/CIO A6 as the Chief Information Officer by law or in AFPD 17-1.

3.2.3. Develop plans and provide guidance to integrate cyberspace operational capabilities with air and space capabilities.

3.3. The AF Director of Test and Evaluation (AF/TE) will:

3.3.1. Develop and implement a comprehensive test strategy, that includes cyber testing, and institute policy consistent with AF and DoD policies.

3.3.2. Ensure AF test and evaluation (T&E) infrastructure utilizes latest cyber intelligence data to provide an operationally representative cyber environment for T&E.

3.4. The Chief of Information Dominance and Chief Information Officer (SAF/CIO A6) will provide policy and guidance to enable an operationally resilient, reliable, and secure cyberspace domain which meets AF operational requirements.

3.5. The General Counsel (SAF/GC) and The Judge Advocate General (AF/JA) will advise the AF on legal matters related to cyberspace operations.

3.6. The Inspector General (SAF/IG) will:

3.6.1. Validate functional inspection criteria to ensure that AF cyberspace capabilities are properly developed in response to documented requirements, and that cyberspace operations are being properly executed.

3.6.2. Through AFOSI, investigate allegations of criminal, fraudulent, and other illegal activities conducted in cyberspace, perform other criminal investigations to protect AF resources in accordance with applicable law, and conduct the full range of cyber counterintelligence activities to protect the AF core missions and enable or engage in cyberspace operations.

3.7. The Administrative Assistant to the Secretary of the Air Force (SAF/AA) will:

3.7.1. Provide oversight and policy authority for cyberspace-related AF special access programs (SAPs) IAW AFPD 16-7, *Special Access Programs*, and AF Instruction (AFI) 16-701, *Management, Administration, and Oversight of Special Access Programs*.

3.7.2. Appoint authorizing officials for AF SAP information systems, platforms, networks, and technologies.

3.8. Air Force Space Command will:

3.8.1. Serve as the core function lead (CFL) for cyberspace superiority.

3.8.2. Issue cyberspace orders on behalf of the Secretary of the Air Force for the overall C2, security and defense of the AFIN; and the C2, implementation, security, operation, maintenance, sustainment, configuration, and defense of the Air Force Network and Air Force Network-Secure (AFNET/AFNET-S).

3.8.3. Manage funds for the AF CMF enterprise.

3.8.4. Present integrated CMF teams to USCYBERCOM through AFCYBER.

3.8.5. Deploy AF-approved cyber weapon systems.

3.9. Air Force Materiel Command will conduct technological research and materiel development activities to acquire, perform developmental testing of, field and sustain current and future cyberspace capabilities.

3.10. Air Education and Training Command will, in coordination with the SAF/CIO A6 Functional Authorities Career Field Managers, develop and implement programs to educate all Airmen on cyberspace operations, the employment of related capabilities, and the integration of those capabilities with capabilities of all other domains.

3.11. The Air Force Operational Test and Evaluation Center (AFOTEC) or MAJCOM Operational Test Units will:

3.11.1. Perform operational test and evaluation (OT&E) in support of cyberspace capabilities development activities.

3.11.2. Execute cyber test policy and guidance as directed by DoD and AF/TE.

3.12. Headquarters AF Functionals, Major Commands, Direct Reporting Units, and Field Operating Agencies will:

3.12.1. Follow AF policy and cyberspace orders when executing cyberspace operations.

3.12.2. Include required cyber testing resources, plans, and measures in all T&E Master Plans to ensure adequate testing of cyber suitability, interoperability, supportability, resiliency, and survivability.

DEBORAH L. JAMES
Secretary of the Air Force

Attachment 1

GLOSSARY OF REFERENCES AND SUPPORTING INFORMATION

References

Presidential Policy Directive 20, *U.S. Cyber Operations Policy,* undated

NIST Special Publication 800-59, *Guideline for Identifying an Information System as a National Security System*, August 2003

DoDD 3700.01, *DoD Command and Control (C2) Enabling Capabilities,* October 22, 2014

DoDD 3710.01, *National Leadership Command Capability (NLCC)*, May 27, 2015

DoDD 8000.01, *Management of the Department of Defense Information Enterprise*, February 10, 2009

DoDD 8100.02, *Use of Commercial Wireless Devices, Services, and Technologies in the Department of Defense (DoD) Global Information Grid (GIG)*, April 14, 2004, certified current as of April 23, 2007

DoDD O-8530.1, *Computer Network Defense (CND),* January 8, 2001

DoDI 3222.03, *DoD Electromagnetic Environmental Effects (E3) Program*, January 8, 2015

DoDI O-3710.02, *Secretary of Defense Communications (SDC),* October 20, 2014

DoDI 4630.09, *Communications Waveform Development and Standardization*, July 15, 2015

DoDI 4650.01, *Policy and Procedures for Management and Use of the Electromagnetic Spectrum*, January 9, 2009

DoDI 4650.02, *Military Auxiliary Radio System (MARS)*, December 23, 2009

DoDI 5000.02, *Operation of the Defense Acquisition System*, January 7, 2015

DoDI 8100.04, *DoD Unified Capabilities (UC)*, December 9, 2010

DoDI 8140.01, *Cyberspace Workforce Management*, August 11, 2015

DoDI 8320.02, *Sharing Data, Information, and Information Technology (IT) Services in the Department of Defense*, August 5, 2013

DoDI 8410.01, *Internet Domain Name Use and Approval*, April 14, 2008

DoDI 8410.02, *NetOps for the Global Information Grid,* December 19, 2008

DoDI 8410.03, *Network Management,* August 29, 2012

DoDI 8500.01, *Cybersecurity*, March 14, 2014

DoDI 8520.02, *Public Key Infrastructure (PKI) and Public Key (PK) Enabling*, May 24. 2011

DoDI 8520.03, *Identity Authentication for Information Systems*, May 13, 2011

DoDI 8523.01, *Communications Security (COMSEC)*, April 22, 2008

DoDI O-8530.2, *Support to Computer Network Defense*, March 9, 2001

CJCSI 3121.01B, *Standing Rules of Engagement/Standing Rules for the Use of Force for US Forces*, June 13, 2005, current as of 18 June 2008.

Joint Publication (JP) 1-02, *Department of Defense Dictionary of Military and Associated Terms*, November 8, 2010, as amended through September 15, 2015

JP 3-12, *Cyberspace Operations*, February 5, 2013

JP 6-0, *Joint Communications System*, June 10, 2015

AFPD 16-7, *Special Access Programs*, February 19, 2014

AFI 16-701, *Management, Administration, and Oversight of Special Access Programs*, February 18, 2014

AFMAN 33-363, *Management of Records*, March 1, 2008

Prescribed Forms

None

Adopted Forms

AF Form 847, *Recommendation for Change of Publication*

Abbreviations and Acronyms

AF —Air Force

AFI —Air Force Instruction

AFIN —Air Force Information Network

AFMAN – Air Force Manual

AFNET – Air Force Network

AFNET-S – Air Force Network-Secure

AFOSI —AF Office of Special Investigations

AFPD —Air Force Policy Directive

AFRIMS —Air Force Records Information Management System

C2 —Command and Control

CFL —Core Function Lead

CIO —Chief Information Officer

CMF —Cyber Mission Force

CND —Computer Network Defense

COMSEC —Communications Security

DCO —Defensive Cyberspace Operations

DoD – Department of Defense

DoDD – Department of Defense Directive

DoDI —Department of Defense Instruction

DoDIN —Department of Defense Information Networks

E3 —Electromagnetic Environmental Effects

GIG —Global Information Grid

ISR —Intelligence, Surveillance, and Reconnaissance

IT —Information Technology

JP —Joint Publication

MARS —Military Affiliate Radio System

NLCC —National Leadership Command Capability

NSS —National Security System

OCO —Offensive Cyberspace Operations

OPR —Office of Primary Responsibility

PD —Policy Directive

PIT— Platform Information Technology

PK —Public Key

PKI —Public Key Infrastructure

RDS —Records Disposition Schedule

SAF —Secretary of the Air Force

SAP —Special Access Program

SCF —Service Core Function

SDC —Secretary of Defense Communications

T&E —Test and Evaluation

TTP —Tactics, Techniques, and Procedures

UC —Unified Capabilities

WLAN —Wireless Local Area Network

Terms

AF Information Network (AFIN) — The globally interconnected, end-to-end set of AF information capabilities, and associated processes for collecting, processing, storing, disseminating, and managing information on-demand to AF warfighters, policy makers, and support personnel, including owned and leased communications and computing systems and services, software (including applications), data, security services, other associated services, and national security systems." (Derived from the JP 3-12 definition of DoDIN).

AFIN Infrastructure—The AF cyberspace infrastructure consisting of AF-owned/leased and controlled components (hardware, software, networks, systems, equipment, facilities, and services) operated by DoD, AF, contractor or other entity on behalf of the AF, which stores, transmits, receives, or processes information, regardless of classification or sensitivity.

AFIN Operations—AF actions taken to design, build, configure, secure, operate, maintain, and sustain AF IT, to include Platform IT (PIT), cyber enabled systems/weapons systems, and National Security Systems (NSS), in a way that creates and preserves data availability, integrity and confidentiality. (Derived from definition of DoDIN Operations).

AF Network (AFNET) —The AF's underlying Nonsecure Internet Protocol Router Network that enables AF operational capabilities and lines of business, consisting of physical medium and data transport services. (Air Force definition).

AF Network-Secure (AFNET-S) — The AF's underlying Secure Internet Protocol Router Network (SIPRNet) that enables AF operational capabilities and lines of business, consisting of physical medium and data transport services. (Air Force definition).

Communications Security (COMSEC)—The protection resulting from all measures designed to deny unauthorized persons information of value that might be derived from the possession and study of telecommunications, or to mislead unauthorized persons in their interpretation of the results of such possession and study. (JP 6-0).

Core Function Lead—SecAF/CSAF-appointed senior leader responsible for specific Core Functions (CF) providing AF-level, long-term views. CFLs integrate Total Force concepts, capabilities, modernization, and resourcing to ensure future assigned core capabilities across the range of military operations as directed by AF Strategy and Strategic Planning Guidance. CFLs are responsible for the Core Function Support Plan and recommendations for the development of the POM for the assigned CF. CFLs have tasking authority regarding CF issues to identify enabling capabilities and integration requirements/opportunities. (AFPD 90-11).

Cyber (adj.) — of or pertaining to the cyberspace environment, capabilities, plans, or operations. (Air Force definition).

Cybersecurity—Prevention of damage to, protection of, and restoration of computers, electronic communications systems, electronic communications services, wire communication, and electronic communication, including information contained therein, to ensure its availability, integrity, authentication, confidentiality, and nonrepudiation. (DoDI 8500.01).

Cyberspace (n. or adj.) — A global domain within the information environment consisting of the interdependent network of information technology infrastructures and resident data, including the Internet, telecommunications networks, computer systems, and embedded processors and controllers. (JP 3-12) NOTE: synonymous with *cyber* when used as an adjective.

Cyberspace Operations — The employment of cyberspace capabilities where the primary purpose is to achieve objectives or effects in or through cyberspace (JP 3-0). Cyberspace Operations are categorized as Offensive Cyberspace Operations (OCO), Defensive Cyberspace Operations (DCO), and DoD Information Networks (DoDIN) Operations (DoDIN Ops). (Described in JP 3-12).

Cyberspace Superiority — The degree of dominance in cyberspace by one force that permits the secure, reliable conduct of operations by that force, and its related land, air, maritime, and space forces at a given time and place without prohibitive interference by an adversary. (JP 3-12).

Defensive Cyberspace Operations (DCO) — Passive and active cyberspace operations intended to preserve the ability to utilize friendly cyberspace capabilities and protect data, networks, and net-centric capabilities, and other designated systems. (JP 3-12).

Defensive Cyberspace Operations —Internal Defensive Measures (DCO-IDM) – Those DCO that are conducted within the DoDIN. They include actively hunting for advanced internal threats as well as the internal responses to those threats. (JP 3-12).

Defensive Cyberspace Operations Response Actions (DCO-RA) — Deliberate, authorized defensive measures or activities taken outside of the defended network to protect and defend DoD cyberspace capabilities or other designated systems. Also called DCO-RA.

Department of Defense Information Networks (DoDIN) — The globally interconnected, end-to-end set of information capabilities, and associated processes for collecting, processing, storing, disseminating, and managing information on-demand to warfighters, policy makers, and support personnel, including owned and leased communications and computing systems and services, software (including applications), data, security services, other associated services, and national security systems. (JP 3-12).

Department of Defense Information Network (DoDIN) Operations—. Operations to design, build, configure, secure, operate, maintain, and sustain Department of Defense networks to create and preserve information assurance on the Department of Defense information networks. (JP 3-12).

Information Dominance. —The operational advantage gained from the ability to collect, control, exploit, and defend information to optimize decision making and maximize warfighting effects. (AF Information Dominance Vision).

Information Technology (IT)—Any equipment, or interconnected system or subsystem of equipment, that is used in the automatic acquisition, storage, manipulation, management, movement, control, display, switching, interchange, transmission, or reception of data or information by the executive agency. This includes equipment used by a Component directly, or used by a contractor under a contract with the Component, which (i) requires the use of such equipment, or (ii) requires the use, to a significant extent, of such equipment in the performance of a service or the furnishing of a product. The term "IT" also includes computers, ancillary equipment, software, firmware and similar procedures, services (including support services), and related resources. Notwithstanding the above, the term "IT" does not include any equipment that is required by a Federal contractor incidental to a Federal contract. Note: The above term is considered synonymous with the term "information system" as defined and used in AF programs. The term "IT" does not include National Security Systems (NSS) according to 44 USC 3502.

National Security System (NSS)—Any information system (including any telecommunications system) used or operated by an agency or by a contractor of an agency, or other organization on behalf of an agency, the function, operation, or use of which involves intelligence activities; involves cryptologic activities related to national security; involves command and control of military forces; involves equipment that is an integral part of a weapon or weapons system; or is critical to the direct fulfillment of military or intelligence missions; or is protected at all times by procedures established for information that have been specifically authorized under criteria established by an Executive order or an Act of Congress to be kept classified in the interest of national defense or foreign policy. (Adapted from NIST SP 800-59 & 44 USC 3542).

Offensive Cyberspace Operations (OCO) — Cyberspace operations intended to project power by the application of force in or through cyberspace. (JP 3-12).

Service Core Functions—Functional areas that delineate the appropriate and assigned core duties, missions, and tasks of the USAF as an organization, responsibility for each of which is assigned to a CFL. SCFs express the ways in which the USAF is particularly and appropriately suited to contribute to national security, although they do not necessarily express every aspect of what the USAF contributes to the nation. (AFPD 90-11).

Platform Information Technology (PIT) — a special purpose system which employs computing resources (i.e., hardware, firmware, and optionally software) that are physically embedded in, dedicated to, or essential in real time to the mission performance. It only performs (i.e., is dedicated to) the information processing assigned to it by its hosting special purpose system (this is not for core services). Examples include, but are not limited to: SCADA type systems, training simulators, diagnostic test and maintenance equipment. (AFI 33-210).

Unified Capabilities (UC)—The integration of voice, video, and/or data services delivered ubiquitously across a secure and highly available network infrastructure, independent of technology, to provide increased mission effectiveness to the warfighter and business communities. (DoDI 8100.04).

Weapon System—A combination of one or more weapons with all related equipment, materials, services, personnel, and means of delivery and deployment (if applicable) required for self-sufficiency. (JP 3-0).

BY ORDER OF THE SECRETARY
OF THE AIR FORCE

AIR FORCE INSTRUCTION 10-1701

5 MARCH 2014

Operations

*COMMAND AND CONTROL (C2) FOR
CYBERSPACE OPERATIONS*

COMPLIANCE WITH THIS PUBLICATION IS MANDATORY

ACCESSIBILITY: Publications and forms are available for downloading or ordering on the e-Publishing website at www.e-Publishing.af.mil

RELEASABILITY: There are no releasability restrictions on this publication

OPR: AF/A3CS/A6CS

Certified by: AF/A3C/A6C
(Maj Gen Earl D. Matthews)
Pages: 15

This Instruction implements Air Force Policy Directive (AFPD) 10-17, *Cyberspace Operations*, and provides guidance for command and control of activities covered in AFI 33-115, *AF IT Services* and supporting Methods and Procedures Technical Orders (e.g., Vulnerability Management MPTO, etc.). This AFI introduces the term *AF Information Networks (AFIN)* as a replacement for the previously-used term AF-GIG. The AFIN is defined as the globally interconnected, end-to-end set of Air Force information capabilities, and associated processes for collecting, processing, storing, disseminating, and managing information on-demand to warfighters, policy-makers, and support personnel, including owned, leased and contracted communications and computing systems and services, software (including applications), data, security services, other associated services, and national security systems. The terms AF Network (AFNET) and AF Network-Secure (AFNET-S) are introduced to refer to the Air Force's underlying Non-Secure Internet Protocol Router Network (NIPRNet) and Secure Internet Protocol Router Network (SIPRNet). This publication applies to all military and civilian AF personnel, members of the AF Reserve Command (AFRC), Air National Guard (ANG), third-party governmental employee and contractor support personnel in accordance with appropriate provisions contained in memoranda support agreements and AF contracts. Violations shall serve as a basis for denying individual's access to the AFIN. The authorities to waive wing/unit level requirements in this publication are identified with a Tier ("T-0, T-1, T-2, T-3") number following the compliance statement. See AFI 33-360, *Publications and Forms Management*, Table 1.1 for a description of the authorities associated with the Tier numbers. Requests for waivers must be submitted through HQ AFSPC/A3 to the OPR listed above for consideration and approval. Refer recommended changes and questions about this publication to the Office of Primary Responsibility (OPR) using the AF Form 847, *Recommendation for Change of Publication*; route AF Form 847s from the field through the appropriate functional's chain of command. This publication may be supplemented at any level, but all direct Supplements must be routed to the OPR of this publication for coordination prior to certification and approval. Ensure that all records created as a result of processes prescribed in this publication are maintained in accordance with AF Manual (AFMAN) 33-363, *Management of Records*, and disposed of in accordance with the Air Force Records Disposition Schedule (RDS) located in the AF Records Information Management System (AFRIMS).

1. General.

1.1. In accordance with AFPD 10-17, the Commander, AF Space Command (AFSPC/CC) is responsible for the overall command and control, security and defense of the AFIN. AFSPC/CC is responsible for the command, control, implementation, security, operation, maintenance, sustainment, configuration, and defense of the AFNET/AFNET-S. Cyber orders issued by AFSPC/CC or his/her delegated representative are military orders issued by order of the Secretary of the Air Force.

1.2. The Unified Command Plan gives the Commander, U. S. Strategic Command (CDRUSSTRATCOM) responsibility to direct operations and defense of the Department of Defense (DoD) Information Networks (DoDIN). CDRUSSTRATCOM, either directly or via Commander, U.S. Cyber Command (USCYBERCOM), issues such orders as required to operate and defend the DoDIN and direct other cyberspace operations as required in support of requesting Combatant Commanders (CCDRs). 24 AF (AFCYBER) is the AF component to USCYBERCOM and, as such, is responsible for ensuring assigned/attached AF forces perform the missions and tasks assigned by USCYBERCOM.

1.3. Command and Control, General.

1.3.1. Classified processes governing C2 of AF offensive and defensive cyberspace operations conducted by AF Cyber Mission Forces are addressed in a classified CJCS Execute Order (title classified) issued on 21 Jun 13.

1.3.2. When necessary to respond to a critical cyber event, as declared by CDRUSSTRATCOM or CDRUSCYBERCOM, AFSPC/CC, his/her delegated representative, or 24 AF/AFCYBER/CC may request applicable AF forces (e.g., Communications Focal Point (CFP) personnel within a Communications Squadron, etc.) be attached for tactical control to 24 AF/AFCYBER for the duration of the event. Due to the immediate nature of most cyber events, approval of the attachment will likely be granted/transmitted verbally or electronically with hard copy orders to follow, per guidance in AFI 38-101, *Air Force Organization*.

1.3.3. All cyber orders must be complied with in the timeline directed. See section 2.2.2 for temporary relief from orders.

1.4. USSTRATCOM/USCYBERCOM issues orders via various formats that include but are not limited to Tasking Orders (TASKORDs) and Operation Orders (OPORDs). Orders received from USCYBERCOM will be relayed promptly, where applicable, through AFCYBER/CC or from his/her delegated representative to the 624 Operations Center (OC) to the tasked units. The 624 OC will relay USCYBERCOM orders to the appropriate units utilizing Cyber Tasking Orders (CTOs), Cyber Control Orders (CCOs), Time Compliance Network Orders (TCNOs), Maintenance Tasking Orders (MTOs), or Special Instructions (SPINS); hereafter referred to as cyber orders. AFCYBER/CC, through the 624 OC, may add AF-specific tasks to an OPORD; however, the original OPORD must remain intact.

1.4.1. Compliance with cyber orders is mandatory. Commanders shall ensure compliance with orders issued pursuant to this instruction and hold personnel and organizations accountable for the consequences of non-compliance **(T-2)**.

1.4.1.1. Military personnel and civilian employees may be subject to administrative and/or judicial sanctions if they knowingly, willfully, or negligently compromise, damage, or place at risk information and information systems by failure to comply with cyber orders issued by AFSPC/CC or his/her delegated representative.

1.4.1.2. Defense contractors are responsible for ensuring employees perform in accordance with the terms of the contracts and applicable directives, laws, and regulations. Violations by contractor personnel will be reported to contracting officers for disposition in accordance with the Federal Acquisition Regulation and applicable contract provisions. Future contracts shall include terms that alert contractors that noncompliance may serve as the basis for revoking access to the AFIN for individual violators, and that noncompliance will be a factor considered in contract performance evaluations **(T-2)**.

1.4.2. Prior to the implementation of this AFI, orders affecting the AFIN were a function of Air Force Network Operations (AFNETOPs). AFNETOPs orders issued prior to the issuance of this AFI remain valid, but orders issued after the date of this instruction will be issued by AFSPC/CC, his/her designated representative, or 24 AF/AFCYBER/CC.

1.5. Types of Orders.

1.5.1. AF CTO. AF CTOs are operational type orders issued to perform specific actions at specific time frames in support of AF and Joint requirements. AF CTOs are generally derived from USCYBERCOM orders and issued by AFCYBER via the 624 OC. AFSPC/CC or his/her delegated representative will issue AF CTOs directly (via 24 AF and the 624 OC) to direct the execution of cyberspace operations to protect and defend the AFIN.

1.5.2. AF CCO. CCOs are used to build/shape the portion of cyberspace to be employed in support of a Combatant Command (CCMD) operation or in response to adversary actions.

1.5.3. AF TCNO. TCNOs are orders issued to direct the immediate patching of information systems to mitigate or eliminate exploitation vulnerabilities. These orders have a significant implication if not accomplished in a timely manner.

1.5.4. AF MTOs. MTOs are routine tasks that enhance network security with a medium to low risk associated with the task.

1.5.5. AF SPINS. SPINS provide amplifying instructions for planning, execution, and assessment of AF CTOs and CCOs.

1.5.6. C4 NOTAMs. Command, Control, Communications, and Computers Notices to Airmen (C4 NOTAMs) are used to disseminate network information that does not direct specific action to be taken or compliance to be tracked.

1.6. AF Cyber Orders Flow Process. Figure 1 graphically depicts the flow of cyber orders.

Figure 1. The AF Cyber Orders Flow Process

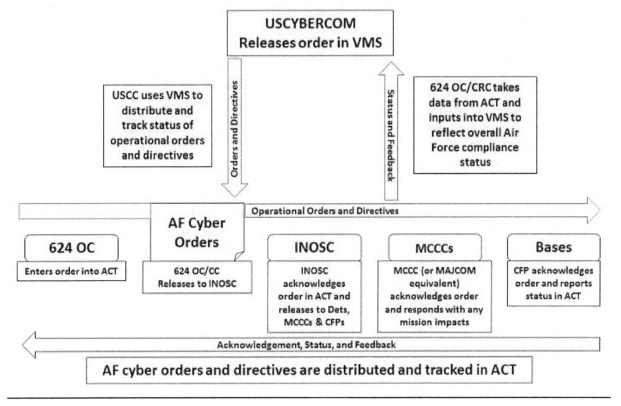

1.6.1. Cyber Orders Distribution. Applicable cyber orders are distributed by the 624 OC to major commands (MAJCOMs), field operating agencies (FOAs), direct reporting units (DRUs), MAJCOM Communications Coordination Centers (MCCCs), AF Component Commands and associated Air Operations Centers (AOCs) and AFFOR Communications Control Centers (ACCCs) for actions affecting assets (e.g., personnel, information systems, etc.) not under the direct control or ownership of 24 AF. For purposes of this Instruction, the term MCCC also includes organizational structures established at the discretion of a MAJCOM which perform the same functions as an MCCC.

1.7. Operational Reports (OPREP). All commanders are required to release OPREPS in accordance with AFI 10-206, *Operational Reporting*. Various cyber events/incidents, especially those impacting mission readiness/capability, will require an OPREP **(T-2)**.

2. Roles and Responsibilities.

2.1. Commander, Air Force Space Command (AFSPC/CC). In accordance with AFPD 10-17, AFSPC/CC is responsible for the overall command and control, security and defense of the AFIN. AFSPC/CC is responsible for the command, control, implementation, security, operation, maintenance, sustainment, configuration, and defense of the AFNET/AFNET-S. These day-to-day authorities may be delegated.

2.2. Commander, Twenty-Fourth Air Force (24 AF (AFCYBER)/CC). 24 AF is the Air Force component to USCYBERCOM. 24 AF/CC, when acting as AFCYBER/CC or when executing authorities delegated by AFSPC/CC, will:

2.2.1. Issue cyber orders as needed for the operation, defense, maintenance and control of the AFIN to Major Commands (MAJCOMs), wings, Integrated Network Operations and Support Centers (I-NOSCs), and CFPs via the 624 OC.

2.2.2. Within established criteria, approve or deny requests from affected organizations for relief from execution of cyber orders if such orders might degrade or impact any unit's ability to successfully complete assigned missions.

2.2.3. Represent AF equities to USCYBERCOM/USSTRATCOM when direction for operation and defense of the AFIN would degrade or impact any AF unit's ability to successfully complete assigned missions. 24 AF/CC (AFCYBER) will coordinate with USCYBERCOM/USSTRATCOM on behalf of affected organizations to resolve such issues.

2.2.4. Coordinate with affected AF organizations and CCDRs DoDIN Operations/defensive cyberspace operations (DCO) organizations to resolve conflicts between USCYBERCOM/USSTRATCOM or AF direction and CCDR direction for AFIN resources supporting CCDR missions.

2.2.5. Present forces to USCYBERCOM and other CCDRs as required in support of cyberspace operations as directed.

2.3. 624th Operations Center (624 OC). The 624 OC is the 24 AF/AFCYBER operations center responsible for issuing cyber orders as directed by 24 AF/AFCYBER/CC. The 624 OC will:

2.3.1. Manage an Air Force-wide tasking system for AF cyber orders as needed. As directed by AFSPC/CC, or if authority has been delegated, by 24 AF (AFCYBER)/CC, the 624 OC will relay USCYBERCOM orders as adopted AF cyber orders to all AF units **(T-2)**.

2.3.2. Relay Air Force and USCYBERCOM cyber orders to appropriate Air Force/AFCYBER units. 624 OC will generate applicable cyber orders to direct AF implementation; however, the original USCYBERCOM orders must remain intact. 624 OC acknowledges receipt of USCYBERCOM orders on behalf of AFCYBER **(T-2)**.

2.3.3. Oversee compliance with AF and USCYBERCOM cyber orders and relay status of those orders to 24 AF/AFCYBER/CC and USCYBERCOM as directed **(T-2)**.

2.3.4. Process requests for relief from AF cyber orders and advise the releasing authority on whether to grant, deny or seek further guidance/direction from USSTRATCOM/USCYBERCOM or AFSPC/CC. If such relief is granted, the 624 OC will immediately and concurrently notify affected organizations **(T-2)**.

2.4. 83rd Network Operations Squadron (NOS), 561st NOS, and 299th Network Operations Security Squadron (NOSS). NOSs receive and disseminate cyber orders from the 624 OC. The NOS unit structure contains the Integrated Network Operations Support Center (I-NOSC) and Enterprise Service Unit (ESU) flights/missions.

2.4.1. Relay, execute, and track cyber orders to affected MAJCOMs, MCCCs, ACCCs, and installation communications units. MAJCOMs, MCCCs and ACCCs pass applicable orders to their installation communications units at MAJCOM discretion or if not already received from the appropriate NOS **(T-2)**.

2.4.2. Coordinate with MAJCOMs, MCCCs, and ACCCs on operational impacts and Plans of Action and Milestones (POA&M) to mitigate risk to the AFIN when compliance with cyber orders cannot be achieved as directed **(T-2)**.

2.4.3. Advise MCCCs, ACCCs, and 624 OC on requests for relief. MCCCs/ACCCs will communicate with their subordinate installation communications units.

2.4.4. The 299 NOSS interfaces with the 624 OC and performs I-NOSC functions for the ANG. In addition to I-NOSC responsibilities the 299 NOSS also acts as the Enterprise Services Unit (ESU), Enterprise Service Desk (ESD) and MCCC for the ANG. 299 NOSS will continue to facilitate the integration of the ANG into the AFIN and work with ANG units to baseline and standardize their systems and equipment in accordance with AF/AFSPC/24 AF AFIN guidance. 299 NOS will:

2.4.4.1. Relay, execute and track cyber orders to ANG CFPs **(T-2)**.

2.4.4.2. Report status of compliance with orders to the 624 OC **(T-2)**.

2.4.4.3. Coordinate with ANG CFPs on operational impacts and POA&M to mitigate risk to the AFIN when relief of orders is granted **(T-2)**.

2.4.4.4. Advise ANG CFPs and the 624 OC on requests for relief **(T-2)**.

2.5. MAJCOMs, MCCCs, ACCCs, Wings, CFPs, and Program Management Offices (PMOs).

2.5.1. Organizational commanders will ensure cyber orders are disseminated to and executed by their subordinate units **(T-2)**. Commanders or their designated representatives may request relief from cyber orders due to operational impacts via 24 AF/AFCYBER-defined orders relief processes **(T-2)**. However, the request does not relieve commanders from implementing cyber orders when capable. Wing Commanders (or equivalent) will keep their respective MAJCOM, MCCCs and ACCCs informed of such requests for relief and expected operational impact if relief is not granted. Wing Commanders over tenant units with operational impact to unique mission systems will request relief through the owning MAJCOM/organization, keeping host base CFP informed **(T-2)**.

2.5.2. MAJCOMs and wings will not normally relay cyber orders to subordinate CFPs. MCCCs and CFPs will receive these orders simultaneously via the 624 OC and supporting I-NOSC. This is only to prevent redundant tasking to the CFPs and does not preclude any commander in the CFPs chain of command from exercising their inherent command authorities. MCCCs will receive cyber orders from the 624 OC and the appropriate I-NOSC and may send them to their installation communications units if not already received from the appropriate NOS.

2.5.3. MAJCOM Communications Coordination Centers. MCCCs provide MAJCOM Commanders and the 624 OC with situational awareness of MAJCOM-unique functional system availability (if applicable) and of compliance with network taskings. In some cases, MCCCs maintain MAJCOM unique functional systems. MCCCs will:

2.5.3.1. Track, assign, and monitor cyber orders issued through the 624 OC and I-NOSCs.

2.5.3.2. Advise the MAJCOM CC on completion of cyber orders or inability to complete assigned tasks pertaining to AFNET, PMO, and MAJCOM-unique systems as required/directed by the MAJCOM/CC.

2.5.3.3. Provide updates on MAJCOM unique network health/status and operational impact to the 624 OC.

2.5.3.4. Advise MAJCOM/CCs, I-NOSC, and 624 OC, on operational impacts of cyber orders to component missions.

2.5.3.5. Coordinate conflicting guidance with I-NOSCs and CCDR DCO organizations.

2.5.3.6. Coordinate Plans of Action and Milestones (POA&M) with I-NOSCs and CCDR DoDIN Ops/DCO organizations to resolve operational impact issues when relief of orders is granted. Ensure POA&Ms are completed for any requests for relief and ensure POA&Ms remain updated and current until compliance with the orders is achieved.

2.5.3.7. Provide situational reports (SITREPS) to their CCDR, MAJCOM and 624 OC related to outage and other network events impacting the AFIN and/or the MAJCOM mission. This requirement does not replace any requirement for OPREP reporting outlined in AFI 10-206.

2.5.4. AFFOR Communications Control Centers. ACCCs support numbered Air Forces (NAF) in their AF and Service component responsibilities. ACCCs provide a similar capability as MCCCs and will:

2.5.4.1. Comply with cyber orders issued by the 624 OC and I-NOSCs.

2.5.4.2. Report completion of cyber orders or inability to complete assigned tasks to the I-NOSCs and 624 OC and their respective MCCC and wing.

2.5.4.3. Provide updates on component unique network activity, health/status, and operational impact to the 624 OC, if applicable.

2.5.4.4. Advise commanders, MCCCs, and 624 OC, on operational impacts of cyber orders to component missions.

2.5.4.5. Coordinate conflicting guidance with I-NOSCs and CCDR DoDIN Ops/DCO organizations.

2.5.4.6. Coordinate POA&Ms with I-NOSCs and CCDR DoDIN Ops/DCO organizations to resolve operational impact issues when relief of orders is granted. Ensure POA&Ms are completed for any requests for relief and ensure POA&Ms remain updated and current until compliance with the orders is achieved.

2.5.4.7. Provide SITREPs to their component and the 624 OC related to outage and other network events impacting the AFIN or the supported CCMD mission.

2.5.5. Communication Focal Points. The base CFPs monitor performance of the local network and serve as the conduit for implementing cyber orders. CFPs will:

2.5.5.1. Direct applicable personnel (e.g., Client System Support Technicians, Functional System Administrators, etc.) to implement cyber orders issued through the 624 OC and I-NOSCs or through the MAJCOMs (e.g. MCCC or similar structure). Provide compliance tracking for all orders that cannot be monitored or tracked electronically **(T-2)**.

2.5.5.2. Report completion of cyber orders or inability to complete assigned tasks that are not electronically visible to their respective wing and MCCC/ACCC. The MCCC/ACCC will report through the appropriate I-NOSC to the 624 OC **(T-2)**.

2.5.5.3. Provide local commanders with situational awareness of their ability to support all required mission areas at their fixed base or deployed location.

2.5.5.4. Coordinate with their parent wing and their respective MCCC/ACCC on operational impacts and POA&Ms to mitigate risk to the AFIN when relief of orders is granted. Ensure POA&Ms are completed for any requests for relief and ensure POA&Ms remain updated and current until compliance with the orders is achieved.

2.5.5.5. CFPs will provide support to tenant organizations of other Services in accordance with the provisions of the applicable Host-Tenant Support Agreement (T-2).

2.5.6. Program Management Offices (PMOs) or PMO-like entities. PMOs or PMO-like entities manage the acquisition and sustainment of information technology, including National Security Systems (NSS). PMO's engineer and deliver platform information technology, automated information systems (AIS), and outsourced information technology (IT). These deliveries may be systems and/or applications based on commercial-off-the-shelf or government-off-the-shelf systems, or a hybrid of each. PMOs ensure compliance with all relative directives and orders. Due to operational/contractual issues, additional testing/validation of software and security updates for PMO systems may be required to ensure engineering, interoperability, and mission functionality is not jeopardized. PMOs will:

2.5.6.1. Comply with cyber orders issued by 624 OC, via the parent MAJCOM/Wing, affecting program systems for which the PMO is responsible.

2.5.6.2. Request relief from cyber orders due to operational impacts, through the appropriate MAJCOM/MCCC to the 624 OC. Systems which cannot meet compliance within six months will be further evaluated for risk to the AFIN, impact to AF missions if quarantined or disconnected from the AFIN, and cost to implement the orders. Within established criteria, 24 AF/CC may accept the risk, require the PMO to implement additional risk mitigating actions and/or recommend to the AFSPC/CC, as the AF DAA, that the system be quarantined or disconnected from the AFIN. Recommendations for quarantine or disconnection due to unacceptable risk may result in a Denial of Authorization to Operate (DATO), per AFI 33-210, *Air Force C&A Process.*

2.5.6.3. Report status of compliance with orders to the appropriate wing, MCCC/ACCC, and to 624 OC.

2.5.6.4. Coordinate POA&Ms through the appropriate wing and/or MCCC/ACCC to the 624 OC on operational impacts and to mitigate risk to the AFIN if relief of orders is granted. Ensure POA&Ms are completed for any requests for relief and ensure POA&Ms remain updated and current until compliance with the orders is achieved. In any case, relief from orders will be governed by the provisions of paragraph 2.5.7.2 above.

2.5.6.5. Update program Technical Orders (TO) as required maintaining compliance with cyber orders. Issue Time Compliance Technical Orders (TCTOs) independent of cyber orders when needed to update TOs in the field pending formal TO change releases.

2.5.6.6. Provide SITREP to the MCCC/ACCC, wing and 624 OC related to outage and other network events impacting the AFIN and/or the MAJCOM mission.

3. Authorized Service Interruptions (ASI).

3.1. ASI Definition. ASIs are scheduled periods of network, equipment, or system downtime required to perform preventive maintenance actions, software or equipment upgrades or replacement, system reboots, etc. There are three defined types of ASIs.

3.1.1. Preventive Maintenance Inspection (PMI). PMI ASIs are required for any preventive maintenance actions accomplished on a recurring basis. Examples include routine maintenance of server equipment or server reboots required due to the application of TCTO/MTO-directed countermeasures.

3.1.2. Routine. Routine ASIs are required for any network system changes that will require an interruption of service to complete. Examples include service interruptions required to perform system/software upgrade, or to repair/replace faulty equipment.

3.1.3. Emergency. Emergency ASIs are for those ad hoc events which require an immediate service interruption to correct hazardous or degraded conditions where loss of human life or of Core Services (DCs, exchange, switches, routers) could occur through lack of immediate action. Examples of emergency outages include power problems, equipment malfunctions, imminent system failures, or any hazardous condition that requires immediate attention and cannot otherwise be scheduled as a routine service interruption.

3.2. Operational Reporting of Mission Impact. Organizations submit OPREPs related to outages IAW AFI 10-206.

3.3. ASI Approval Authority.

3.3.1. The AFSPC/CC or, when authority has been delegated, 24 AF/CC, is the approval authority for routine and emergency ASI requests associated with those AFIN links, nodes, functional systems, or services on the AFIN (1) directly supporting an active CCMD operation; (2) whose compromise or loss could affect national security; or (3) whose compromise or loss would degrade or disable critical C2 communications. The 624 OC is the focal point for the coordination of ASIs that must be approved by both the affected installation commander and the 24 AF/CC.

3.3.2. The installation commander is the approval authority for all PMI ASI requests that do not impact the AFNET/AFNET-S or meet the criteria specified in paragraph 3.3.1 **(T-2)**.

3.4. General ASI Coordination Guidance.

3.4.1. Service interruptions will be scheduled at a time that will have the minimum impact on operations **(T-2)**.

3.4.2. Requesting organizations must complete applicable local level coordination (e.g., major tenant unit commanders) on all ASIs prior to submitting the ASI request for approval.

4. Periods of Non-Disruption (PONDs).

4.1. PONDs are directed by USCYBERCOM to halt all maintenance actions within either a geographic or functional Area of Responsibility (AOR), or for very specific systems and or assets crossing one or more AORs. PONDS are intended to ensure commanders have full availability of critical C2 capabilities.

4.2. PONDs will only be issued to support real-world operations, crisis situations, and significant events that may negatively impact national security.

4.3. Requests for PONDs will be channeled through the ASI coordination chain to USCYBERCOM for final approval/disapproval.

BURTON M. FIELD, Lt Gen, USAF
DCS Operations, Plans & Requirements

Attachment 1

GLOSSARY OF REFERENCES AND SUPPORTING INFORMATION

References

CJCSI 3121.01B, *Standing Rules Of Engagement/Standing Rules For The Use Of Force For US Forces*, 13 June 2005 (Current as of 18 Jun 08)

CJCSI 6510.01F, *Information Assurance (IA) and Support to Computer Network Defense (CND)*, 9 February 2011

CJCSM 6510.01A, *Information Assurance (IA) and Computer Network Defense (CND) Volume I (Incident Handling Program)*, 24 Jun 09

CJCS Execute Order, *Title Classified*, 21 June 2013

DoDD O-8530.1-M, DoD *Computer Network Defense (CND) Service Provider Certification and Accreditation Process,* January 8, 2001

DoDD 3600.01, *Information Operations*, August14, 2006, with Change 1, 23 May 2011

DoDI 8510.01, *DoD Information Assurance Certification and Accreditation Process (DIACAP)*, 28 November 2007

DoDD O-8530.1, *Computer Network Defense (CND)*, 8 January 2001

DoDI O-8530.2, *Support to Computer Network Defense (CND)*, 9 March 2001

JP 1-02, *DoD Dictionary of Military and Associated Terms*, As Amended Through 15 May 2011

JP 3-12, *Cyberspace Operations (U)*, SECRET/REL USA, FVEY, 5 February 2013

AFDD 3-12, *Cyberspace Operations*, 15 July 2010, w/change 1, 30 November 2011

AFPD 10-17, *Cyberspace Operations*, 31 July 2012

AFI 10-206, *Operational Reporting*, 6 September 2011

AFI 10-701, *Operations Security,* 8 June 2011

AFI 10-710, *Information Operations Condition (INFOCON)*, 10 August 2006

AFI 33-150, *Management of Cyberspace Support Activities*, 30 November 2011

AFI 33-210, *Air Force C&A Process*, 28 Dec 2008

AFI 38-101, *Air Force Organization*, 16 Mar 11

AFMAN 33-363, *Management of Records*, 1 March 2008

TO 00-33A-1001, *General Communications Activities Management Procedures and Practice Requirements*, 1 December 2012

TO 00-33A-1109, *AF-GIG Vulnerability Management*, 9 January 2013

Adopted Forms

AF Form 847, *Recommendation for Change of Publication*

Abbreviations and Acronyms

24 AF/CC—Commander, Twenty-Fourth Air Force

624 OC—624th Operations Center

ACCC—AFFOR Communications Control Centers

ACT—AFNETOPS Compliance Tracker

AFDD—Air Force Doctrine Document

AFFOR—Air Force Forces

AFI—Air Force Instruction

AFIN—Air Force Information Networks

AFMAN—Air Force Manual

AFPD—Air Force Policy Directive

AFRC—Air Force Reserve Command

ANG—Air National Guard

C2—Command and Control

C4 NOTAM—Command, Control, Communications, and Computer Notice to Airmen

CC—Commander

CCDR—Combatant Commander

CCO—Cyberspace Control Order

CCS—Command & Control Squadron

CDRUSCYBERCOM—Commander, United States Cyber Command

CDRUSSTRATCOM—Commander, United States Strategic Command

CFP—Communications Focal Point

CJCSI—Chairman, Joint Chiefs of Staff Instruction

C-MAJCOM—Component MAJCOM

C-NAF—Component NAF

CND—Computer Network Defense

CTO—Cyber Tasking Order

DoD—Department of Defense

DoDD—Department of Defense Directive

DoDI—Department of Defense Instruction

DoDIN—Department of Defense Information Networks

DRU—Direct Reporting Unit

ESD—Enterprise Service Desk

ESU—Enterprise Services Unit

FOA—Field Operating Agency

I-NOSC—Integrated NOSC

IT—Information Technology

JFC—Joint Force Commander

JP—Joint Publication

MAJCOM—Major Command

MCCC—MAJCOM Communications Coordination Center

MTO—Maintenance Tasking Order

NAF—Numbered Air Force

NOS—Network Operations Squadron

NOSC—Network Operations & Security Center

NOSS—Network Operations and Security Squadron

OC—Operations Center

OPORD—Operation Order

OPR—Office of Primary Responsibility

PMO—Program Management Office

POA&M—Plan of Actions and Milestones

SPINS—Special Instructions

TCNO—Time Compliance Network Order

TCTO—Time Compliance Technical Order

TO—Technical Order

USCYBERCOM—United States Cyber Command

VMS—Vulnerability Management System

Terms

Air Force Forces (AFFOR)— United States Air Force component command assigned to a Joint Force Commander (JFC) at the unified, sub unified, and Joint Task Force (JTF) level. AFFOR includes the COMAFFOR-cyberspace operations, his/her staff, 624 OC, and all Air Force forces and personnel assigned to attach to that Joint Force's Air Force component.

Air Force Information Networks (AFIN)— The globally interconnected, end-to-end set of Air Force information capabilities, and associated processes for collecting, processing, storing, disseminating, and managing information on-demand to warfighters, policy-makers, and support personnel, including owned and leased communications and computing systems and services, software (including applications), data, security services, other associated services, and national security systems.

Air Force Network (AFNET)— The Air Force's underlying Nonsecure Internet Protocol Router Network (NIPRnet) that enables Air Force operational capabilities and lines of business, consisting of physical medium and data transport services. Includes transmission mediums, gateways, routers, switches, hubs and firewalls, and the functions required to support and enable the environment such as command and control, management, maintenance, network authentication, and defense. (AFSPC Commander's Intent)

Air Force Network—Secure (AFNET-S) - The Air Force's underlying Secure Internet Protocol Router Network (SIPRnet) that enables Air Force operational capabilities and lines of business, consisting of physical medium and data transport services. Includes transmission mediums, gateways, routers, switches, hubs and firewalls, and the functions required to support and enable the environment such as command and control, management, maintenance, network authentication, and defense. (AFSPC Commander's Intent)

Commander, Air Force Forces (COMAFFOR)— Designated whenever US Air Force forces are presented to a joint commander. In any operation, a COMAFFOR is designated from the US Air Force and serves as the commander of US Air Force forces assigned and attached to the Joint Force Air Component. (AFDD 2).

Communications Focal Point (CFP)— The consolidation of help desk, telephone trouble tickets and Maintenance Operations Center. This function tracks all communications systems/equipment outages and resides with the Client Service Center (CSC) work center.

Computer Network Defense (CND)— Actions taken to protect, monitor, analyze, detect, and respond to unauthorized activity within Department of Defense information systems and computer networks. (JP 6-0). This term is being replaced by Defensive Cyberspace Operations (DCO).

Cyber (adj.)— Of or pertaining to the cyberspace environment, capabilities, plans, or operations. (AFPD 10-17)

Cyber Tasking Order (CTO)— An operational type order issued to perform specific actions at specific time frames in support of AF and Joint requirements.

Cyber Orders— A general term used to refer to the various types of orders issued for network operations and maintenance (CTOs, CCOs, SPINS, MTOs, etc).

Cyberspace— A global domain within the information environment consisting of the interdependent network of information technology infrastructures, including the Internet, telecommunications networks, computer systems, and embedded processors and controllers. (JP 1-02)

Cyberspace Control Order (CCO)— Used to build/shape the portion of cyberspace to be employed in support of a CCMD operation or in response to adversary actions.

Cyberspace Operations— The employment of cyber capabilities where the primary purpose is to achieve military objectives or effects in or through cyberspace. (AFPD 10-17)

Cyberspace Support— Foundational, continuous or responsive operations in order to ensure information integrity and availability in, through, or from Air Force-controlled infrastructure and its interconnected analog and digital portion of the battlespace. (AFDD 3-12)

Department of Defense Information Networks (DoDIN)— The globally interconnected, end-to-end set of information capabilities, and associated processes for collecting, processing, storing, disseminating, and managing information on-demand to warfighters, policy makers, and support personnel, including owned and leased communications and computing systems and services, software (including applications), data, security services, other associated services, and national security systems. (Joint Pub 3-12)

Department of Defense Information Networks Operations (DoDIN Ops)— Operations to design, build, configure, secure, operate, maintain, and sustain Department of Defense networks to create and preserve information assurance on the Department of Defense information networks. (Joint Pub 3-12)

Information Operations (IO)— The integrated employment, during military operations, of information-related capabilities in concert with other lines of operation to influence, disrupt, corrupt, or usurp the decision-making of adversaries and potential adversaries while protecting our own. Also called IO. (JP 1-02)

Maintenance Tasking Order (MTO)— Routine tasks that enhance network security with a medium to low risk associated with the task.

Operation Order (OPORD). A directive issued by a commander to subordinate commanders for the purpose of effecting the coordinated execution of an operation. (JP 5—0)

Special Instructions (SPINS)—. Provide amplifying instructions for planning, execution, and assessment of AF CTOs and CCOs.

Time Compliance Network Order (TCNO)— A downward-directed operations, security or configuration management-related order issued by USCYBERCOM in an Operational Order (OPORD). TCNOs do not replace information conditions (INFOCONs), Operational Event/Incident Reports (OPREPs), SITREPs or Time Compliance Technical Orders (TCTO). The TCNO provides a standardized mechanism to issue an order.

DEPARTMENT OF THE AIR FORCE
WASHINGTON, DC

MEMORANDUM FOR DISTRIBUTION C
                MAJCOMs/FOAs/DRUs

FROM: SAF/CIO A6
         1800 Air Force Pentagon
         Washington, DC 20330-1800

SUBJECT: Air Force Guidance Memorandum to Air Force Instruction 33-200, *Air Force Cybersecurity Program Management*

ACCESSIBILITY: Publication is available for downloading on the e-Publishing web site at www.e-Publishing.af.mil.

RELEASABILITY: There are no releasability restrictions on this publication.

By Order of the Secretary of the Air Force, this Guidance Memorandum articulates direction to enforce Air Force personnel and contractor compliance with cybersecurity policies and standards. Compliance with this Memorandum is mandatory. To the extent its directions are inconsistent with other Air Force publications; the information herein prevails in accordance with Air Force Instruction 33-360, *Publications and Forms Management*.

Unless otherwise noted, the SAF/CIO A6 is the waiver authority to policies contained in this AFGM. Ensure that all records created as a result of processes prescribed in this publication are maintained as evidentiary documents supporting annual financial audits, or otherwise maintained and disposed of in in accordance with Air Force Manual 33-363, *Management of Records*, and the Air Force Records Disposition Schedule located in the Air Force Records Information Management System.

This memorandum provides guidance concerning This guidance has been incorporated into the upcoming publication Air Force Instruction 17-130, *Air Force Cybersecurity Program Management*. *Disciplinary Actions*

Air Force Information Technology user's behaviors are monitored to detect potentially unauthorized activity, and punitive methods and procedures will be applied in cases where Air Force uniformed, civilian, or contractor personnel are found in violation of applicable cybersecurity laws, policies and/or standards. **Failure to observe the prohibitions and mandatory provisions of this instruction as stated in Section 6 by military personnel is a violation of the *Uniform Code of Military Justice (UCMJ)*, Article 92, Failure to Obey Order or Regulation. Violations by civilian employees may result in administrative**

disciplinary action without regard to otherwise applicable criminal or civil sanctions for violations of related laws. Violations by contactor personnel will be handled according to local laws and the terms of the contract. Additionally violations of Section 6 by ANG military personnel may subject members to prosecution under their respective State Military Code or result in administrative disciplinary action without regard to otherwise applicable criminal or civil sanctions for violations of related laws.

The following guidance applies:

Implementation.

The following language will supersede the language found in Air Force Instruction 17-102, *Communications and Information Specialized Publications*, and Air Force Manual 17-1201, (formerly Air Force Manual 33-152), *User Responsibilities and Guidance for Information Systems*.

1. *General Protection*

    1.1. All authorized users will protect networked and/or stand-alone ISs against tampering, theft, and loss. Protect information systems from insider and outsider threats by controlling physical access to the facilities and data by implementing procedures identified in Joint, Department of Defense, Air Force publications, and organizationally created procedures.

    1.1.1. Backing up personal data stored locally on Air Force Information Technology (e.g. desktop computer, laptop) is the responsibility of the user. Local organizational policy dictates frequency and limitation factors.

2. *Cybersecurity Training*

    2.1. All IS users will complete Department of Defense cybersecurity training prior to granting access to an information system according to Department of Defense Manual 8570.01-M, *IA Workforce Improvement Program*.

    2.2. Users re-perform cybersecurity training annually using the Advanced Distributed Learning System computer based training which reports compliance to the Information System Security Officer.

    2.3. When a user requires a new account or modification to an existing account (due to change of station or assignment, Temporary Duty, etc.), users are not required to retake the Department of Defense Cybersecurity training provided the user has a valid and current (within a year) course completion record.

3. *Access Control*

    3.1. Physical and logical access to all Air Force Information Technology must be mediated using the most reliable and secure technology available, consistent with risk, Air Force standards, and operational requirements.

3.2. Air Force Information Technology information systems must:

3.2.1. Enforce information flows:

3.2.1.1. Air Force Information Technology must adhere to a Discretionary Access Control architecture, supported by a Role Based Access Control model when technically feasible.

3.2.1.2. Information at a lower level of sensitivity or classification may be written up to a container holding information at a higher level of sensitivity or classification. Information at a higher level of sensitivity or classification must not be written down to a container holding information at a lower level of sensitivity or classification, except through a controlled interface such as Defense Information Systems Agency-approved High Assurance Guard, or when the system or systems is/are accredited and authorized to operate in a multilevel mode.

3.2.2. Be configured to limit unsuccessful access attempts by locking the Air Force Information Technology asset after no less than three number of attempts until released by an administrator. Waivers and modifications to this standard may be granted by the cognizant Authorizing Official via record correspondence.

3.2.3. Display the AF-wide standard acceptable use banner upon login that requires user acknowledgment before granting access to Air Force Information Technology resources.

3.2.4. Conspicuously display an on-screen classification banner that is continuously visible while the system is logged into. Systems that do not feature a user screen or monitor must be physically tagged to indicate the highest level of classification that the device can process, transmit, display or store.

3.2.5. Be configured to initiate a session lock in accordance with applicable STIGs/SRGs, or after 10 minutes of inactivity, whichever is more restrictive, and terminate the session in accordance with applicable Security Technical Implementation Guides /Security Requirements Guides, or after 2 hours of inactivity, whichever is more restrictive. Units may instantiate stricter standards at their discretion, consistent with risk and mission needs. Waivers to relax these standards may be granted by the cognizant Authorizing Official via record correspondence.

3.3. Remote access to the Air Force Information Network for telework and remote administration is permitted, with the following conditions and restrictions:

3.3.1. Criteria for determining eligibility for telework are identified in Department of Defense Instruction 1035.01, *Telework Policy*, and Air Force Instruction 36-816, *Civilian Telework Program*. User's remote access must be approved in advance by cognizant management, employing the DD Form 2946, *DoD Telework Agreement*.

3.3.2. Remote access and processing is allowed only at the unclassified level unless explicitly authorized by the cognizant command and cognizant Authorizing Official.

3.3.2.1. If classified telework is authorized at an approved alternative secure location, users must comply with procedures established by Air Force regarding such work. Refer to Air Force Instruction 31-401, *Information Security Program Management*, for guidance on Information Protection.

3.3.2.2. Remote privileged access (e.g., for remote administration) must be justified, with the rationale for allowing such access documented in detail in the remote access agreement. Curt, non-descriptive rationales such as "needed for work" or "system administrator" are not acceptable.

3.3.3. All remote access connections must be effected through a managed access point, and must be protected using Air Force-authorized Virtual Private Network technology, in accordance with DISA Remote Access Policy, Remote Endpoint, and Remote Access Virtual Private Network Security Technical Implementation Guides.

3.3.4. Remote access to the Air Force Information Network is allowed from external systems, e.g., systems owned, administered, maintained and operated by organizations external to Air Force, to include other DoD, federal state, local, tribal, non-governmental and contractor organizations. The guidance in this section does not apply to the use of external information systems to access public interfaces to Air Force Information Technology; otherwise, the following conditions and restrictions apply:

3.3.4.1. Third-parties' systems access must be governed through a formal third-party agreement between Air Force and the owner of the external system, e.g. law, policy, contract, Memorandums of Agreement or Understanding. Air Force and its third-party partners will each retain a copy of the agreement. Department of Defense Instruction 4000.19, *Third Party Agreements*, is germane.

3.3.4.2. Third party agreements must explicitly specify the terms and conditions under which an external system may be allowed to access Air Force Information Technology resources. Terms and conditions may be more restrictive, but cannot be less restrictive, than the terms of this Instruction. In cases where less restrictive controls are necessitated by business/mission requirements, third party access must be confined to a Demilitarized Zone.

3.3.4.3. In cases where responsibility for security control implementation, maintenance, and monitoring are shared between and a third party, the division of responsibilities must be explicitly addressed in the third party agreement.

3.3.4.4. Compliance with the terms of third-party agreements must be included in the RMF authorization package, and included in the continuous monitoring regime.

3.3.5. Remote access requires two-factor authentication; the requirement for two-factor authentication is mandatory, with no waivers allowed. Attachment 8, *AF Public Key Infrastructure and Public Key Enabling*, is germane.

4. Account Management

4.1. All Air Force Information Technology will identify and maintain user accounts to control access and maintain personal accountability.

4.2. All organizations owning or operating Air Force Information Technology will:

4.2.1. Ensure that account management guidance and processes are properly reflected in system security plans.

4.2.2. Identify and define account types[1] (e.g., non-privileged, privileged, guest, maintenance) to support organizational missions/business functions for Air Force Information Technology under their cognizance.

4.2.3. Actively manage Air Force Information Technology accounts; for each account type, authorized users must be specified, group and role membership conditions/requirements defined, and access authorizations/privileges and other attributes (as required) assigned. Attachment 4, *Access Control* and Attachment 6, *Identification and Authentication*, are germane.

4.2.4. Develop procedures for managing the user account life cycle; procedures must define the circumstances and actions to be taken to create, enable, modify, suspend, disable and remove/retire user accounts.

4.3. Formal approvals are required for account establishment using the DD Form 2875; each users' workplace supervisor must specify and justify the privileges to be granted, and the cognizant Information Owner, Information System Security Officer, and Information System Security Manager must approve. See also Attachment 7, *Segregation of Duties and Least Privilege* for details on privilege management.

4.3.1. Electronic DD 2875s and associated documents are preferred over hard copy, digital signatures are preferred over wet signatures.

4.3.2. Section 5.2.14 describes alternative requirements for organizations with high PERSTEMPO, e.g. schoolhouses and training commands.

4.4. Access and privilege authorizations must be based on:

4.4.1. A valid need-to-access/need-to-know; users requiring elevated/administrative/ cybersecurity privileges on information system accounts will receive additional scrutiny by account approval authorities.

4.4.2. Intended system usage.

4.4.3. Other attributes as required by missions/business functions.

4.5. Foreign Nationals. Non-U.S. citizens/permanent residents may be provisioned with accounts granting access to Air Force Information Technology and associated networks

---

[1] Account types will vary widely by system, and should reflect and support each systems' mission.

and resources in accordance with the requirements of this Attachment, in addition to the following requirements and conditions:

4.5.1. The subject Foreign National must be covered by a valid host-nation agreement.

4.5.2. Foreign National clearance and need-to-know must be validated prior to account establishment. in accordance with DoD 5200.02-R, *Personnel Security Program*, only U.S. citizens are eligible for a security clearance; however, compelling reasons may exist to grant access to classified information to an immigrant alien or a foreign national using a "Limited Access Authorization". Department of Defense Directive 5230.11, *Disclosure of Classified Military Information to Foreign Governments and International Organizations*, and Department of Defense Directive 5230.20, *Visits and Assignments of Foreign Nationals* are also germane.

4.5.3. FN access to Air Force Information Technology must be addressed in accessed systems' Risk Managed Framework assessment package(s).

4.6. Modification of existing accounts must take into account the principles of least privilege and segregation of duties; see Attachment 6. Modification procedures must be designed to guard against 'privilege creep', i.e., allowing users to acquire more and more privileges to gain excessive control over a mission/business process.

4.7. Accounts must be suspended or disabled when:

4.7.1. A user is assigned to temporary duty and cannot be expected to employ their authorized account for a period of 45 or more days.

4.7.2. An account is idle for 45 or more days; idle account suspensions must be automated.

4.7.3. An authorized user transfers or retires.

4.7.4. A user is suspected of conduct that could result in their reassignment, removal, or dismissal. In such cases, the account can be reactivated upon cognizant management approval.

4.8. Accounts must be removed/retired no more than:

4.8.1. Thirty (30) days after an authorized user transfers or retires. Key files and logs must be saved or transferred prior to account removal.

4.8.2. Ten (10) days after a user is moved into a different group/role or their need-to-know changes. Key files and must be saved or transferred prior to account removal.

4.9. Account management procedures must address the use of temporary accounts as a part of normal account activation, when there is a need for short-term accounts without the demand for immediacy in account activation. Temporary accounts must be suspended when no longer needed, but are not subject to automatic suspension/deletion.

4.10. Account management procedures must address account creation and suspension/deletion for deployed organizations and Air Force Information Technology; a process for reissuing shared/group account credentials when individuals are removed from the group must be designed and implemented.

4.11. Account management procedures must address account creation and suspension/deletion in emergency circumstances, as described below:

4.11.1. Emergency accounts will be created only under circumstances that could otherwise result in substantial mission degradation or mission failure; they must not be used for administrative convenience.

4.11.2. Emergency account establishment procedures may bypass normal account authorization processes, however, a chain of accountability must be maintained.

4.11.3. Emergency account justifications must detail the potential impacts resulting from failure to establish such accounts.

4.11.4. Emergency accounts must be assigned to individuals; group emergency accounts are proscribed.

4.11.5. All actions performed through emergency accounts must be logged, and logs examined by cognizant personnel.

4.11.6. Emergency accounts must be suspended and/or deleted within an organizationally defined time period, but are not subject to automatic suspension/deletion. Key files and logs must be saved or transferred to another user prior to account removal.

4.12. Account management procedures must address account creation and suspension/deletion in exigent circumstances, as described below:

4.12.1. Accounts terminated under hostile/adverse circumstances must be designed to limit/prevent any harmful measure that may be taken by the terminated user, and to ensure the availability and integrity of suspended users files and audit trails for business continuity and/or damage assessment purposes; a minimum of 90 previous calendar days' worth relevant files and audit trails must be preserved and transferred to cybersecurity personnel and/or law enforcement.

4.13. All Air Force Information Technology capable of doing so will automatically audit for and notify account managers of account creation, modification, enabling, disabling, and removal actions.

4.14. Systems that feature automated mechanisms to support the management of information system accounts are preferred.

4.15. Air Force organizations that experience a high PERSTEMPO by virtue of their mission (schoolhouses, training commands, etc.) may employ the following techniques to ease the administrative burden of managing DD Form 2875s, as described in the following sections:

4.15.1. Create an attachment that contains the names of all Temporary Duty/ Temporary Additional Duty population members and the role(s)/privileges they are authorized. If different members among the population will be granted access to different roles/privileges, indicate the relevant role(s)/privileges next to each name.

4.15.1.1. In circumstances where Temporary Duty/Temporary Additional Duty personnel arrive aperiodically rather than simultaneously in a class/cadre structure, create an attachment that is revised every 1-6 months, depending on PERTEMPO.

4.15.2. Have the individual in the Supervisor role sign and provide a date-time group the attachment document.

4.15.3. For each system and temporary user population, create and process a single DD Form 2875 that is signed by all required authorities.

4.15.4. In Block 13, enter the justification for the entire population requiring access. The justification description may be brief, but not perfunctory; entries such as "Students" or "Needed for course" are not acceptable.

4.15.5. Enter the Supervisor name and Attachment date-time group into Block 13; attach the relevant Attachment to the DD 2875 and file.

4.15.6. After the temporary users have completed their class/training, delete their access and so note it on the DD 2875.

4.15.7. Retain the DD 2875 and attachment for a minimum of one year.

5. *Monitoring Warnings*

5.1. Users of Department of Defense telecommunications devices are to be notified the use of these systems constitutes consent to monitoring.

5.1.1. All users of Department of Defense information systems will sign the standardized Air Force Form 4394. Local organizational commanders must restrict access to Department of Defense information systems for those personnel who fail to sign the agreement. Organization Information System Security Officers are required to report to the Enterprise Service Desk any failures to sign the agreement for revocation of access to enterprise capabilities.

5.1.2. To maintain continuous notifications to all users using Department of Defense telecommunications devices including Voice over Internet Protocol phone instruments, user will report to the Information System Security Officer any of following deficiencies:

5.1.2.1. A DD Form 2056, *Telephone Monitoring Notification Decal*, is missing or not readable on the front of all official telephones and VoIP phone instruments.

5.1.2.2.   A DD Form 2056 is missing or not readable on fax machines.

5.1.2.3.   Locally created organizational/unit fax cover sheets do not contain the exact notice and consent statement: *"Do not transmit classified information over unsecured telecommunications systems. Official Department of Defense telecommunications systems are subject to monitoring. Using Department of Defense telecommunications systems constitutes consent to monitoring."*

6. *Controlled Unclassified Information Handling*

6.1.   Controlled Unclassified Information must be encrypted for transmission; this includes, but is not limited to:

6.1.1.   Information exempted from the terms of the Freedom of Information Act (For Official Use Only. Marking: FOUO).

6.1.2.   Information protected under the terms of information that is Personally Identifiable Information as defined in OMB Memo 17-12 and AFI 33-332 (Personally Identifiable Information. Marking: PRVCY or PII).

6.1.3.   Information protected under the terms of the Health Insurance Portability and Accountability Act or protected health information (Protected Health Information. Marking: HLTH or PHI).

6.1.3.1.   Proprietary Business Information. (Marking: PROPIN).

6.1.3.2.   Procurement and Acquisition Information. (Marking: PROCURE)

6.1.3.3.   Controlled Technical Information (Marking: CTI).

6.1.3.4.   Critical Infrastructure Information (Marking CRIT).

6.1.3.5.   Emergency Management (Marking: EMGT)

6.1.3.6.   Export Control Information (Marking: EXPT).

6.1.3.7.   Government Financial/Fiscal Functions (Marking: FNC).

6.1.3.8.   Geodetic Product Information (Marking: GEO).

6.1.3.9.   Information Systems Vulnerability Information (Marking: ISVI).

6.1.3.10.   International Agreements (Marking: INTL).

6.1.3.11.   Legal and Law Enforcement Information (Marking: LEI)

6.1.3.12.   Nuclear Information (Marking: NUC).

6.1.3.13.   Transportation – Sensitive Security Information (Marking: SSI).

See *www.archives.gov/cui* for further information and a complete list.

6.2.   Controlled Unclassified Information must not be transmitted on or to any system not approved for that information, to include Air Force Information Technology or other

DoD-subordinated; federal, state or local civil government; tribal; non-governmental, contractor, or private systems.

6.3.   Controlled Unclassified Information transmitted through a commercial or wireless network (e.g., remote office, mobile hotspot, commercial Internet café) must be transmitted through an encrypted Virtual Private Network connection or other authorized encryption solution whenever practical. Contact the Enterprise Service Desk or the cognizant base Communications Focal Point for instructions on installation and usage.

6.4.   When transmitting Controlled Unclassified Information, add "CUI" to the beginning of the subject line, followed by the subject. Apply the following statement at the beginning of the message: "*CONTROLLED UNCLASSIFIED INFORMATION. Unauthorized disclosure or misuse of this information may result in criminal and/or civil penalties.*" Additional protection methods may include password protecting the information in a separate portable document format supporting password protection.

6.4.1.   Transmitting information exempt from public release under the Freedom of Information Act must be marked "CUI" at the beginning of the subject line in accordance with guidance contained in this Instruction. Apply the following statement at the beginning of the message: "*FOR OFFICIAL USE ONLY. Unauthorized disclosure or misuse of this information may result in criminal and/or civil penalties.*"

6.4.1.1.   Do not send Freedom of Information Act-exempted information in electronic messages without an appropriate level of protection to prevent unintentional or unauthorized disclosure. Refer to this Instruction for additional guidance or consult the cognizant local FOIA representative. Appropriate level of protection includes proper marking and encryption.

6.4.1.2.   Transmitting personal information exempt from public release under the terms of the Privacy Act of 1974 must be marked "CUI" at the beginning of the subject line in accordance with guidance contained in this Instruction and Air Force Instruction 33-332. Apply the following statement at the beginning of the message: "*The information herein is Controlled Unclassified Information (CUI) which must be protected under the Privacy Act of 1974, as amended. Unauthorized disclosure or misuse of this PERSONAL INFORMATION may result in criminal and/or civil penalties.*"

6.4.1.3.   Do not send Privacy Act information to distribution lists or group email addresses unless each member has an official need to know for the personal information.

6.4.1.4.   This statement must not be applied to messages that are not publically releasable. Use it only in situations when you are actually transmitting personal information. Personal information may not be disclosed to anyone outside Department of Defense unless specifically authorized by The Privacy Act.

6.4.1.5.   Transmitting personal and or medically-related information exempt from public release under the terms of the Health Insurance Portability and Accountability Act must be marked "CUI" at the beginning of the subject line. Apply the following statement at the beginning of the message: *"The information herein is Controlled Unclassified Information (CUI) which must be protected under the Health Insurance Portability and Accountability Act, as amended. Unauthorized disclosure or misuse of this PROTECTED HEALTH INFORMATION may result in criminal and/or civil penalties."*

6.5.   Controlled Unclassified Information must not be copied or posted on Department of Defense-owned, -operated, or -controlled publically accessible sites or on commercial Internet-based capabilities.

6.6.   To the greatest practical extent, Air Force Information Technology and contractor-owned information technology displaying Controlled Unclassified Information must be physically positioned so that the information is not viewable by unauthorized individuals.

6.7.   Loss or suspected loss of removable media containing Controlled Unclassified Information must be reported immediately in accordance with guidance contained in this Instruction and Air Force Instruction 33-332, *Air Force Privacy Program*.

7.   *Configuration Management*

7.1.   Configuration management processes must be institutionalized and documented throughout Air Force systems' life cycles – see Undersecretary of Defense - Acquisition, Training and Logistics MIL-HDBK-61A(SE), *Configuration Management*, for further guidance. **(T-1)**. Personnel with cognizance over configuration management processes must ensure that:

7.1.1.   All Configuration Items are identified and memorialized; the Configuration Item list/database itself must be controlled as a Configuration Item.

7.1.2.   The development, test and promotion to production of their respective systems are governed by a formal Systems Development Life Cycle process; strict segregation of these environments must be maintained in accordance with Attachment 7, *Segregation of Duties and Least Privilege*.

7.1.3.   The development and modification of system Configuration Items, including software, hardware, firmware, data and files, is governed by a Configuration Control Board that reviews, assesses, and approves at its discretion all proposed changes to Configuration Items, and ensures:

7.1.4.   That the current, approved collection of Configuration Items is maintained as a formal baseline.

7.1.5.   That system-specific change management standards and procedures are developed, approved, promulgated and enforced.

7.1.6.   Air Force information technology must be configured to provide only essential capabilities, and prohibit or restrict the use of formally defined/proscribed functions, ports, protocols, and/or services in accordance with Department of Defense Instruction 8551.01 and Air Force System Security Instruction 8551, *Ports, Protocols, and Services Management (PPSM)*.

7.1.7.   Security configuration and implementation decisions will be guided by relevant Federal and Department of Defense guidance, such as National Institute for Standards and Technology Special Publications, Defense Information Systems Agency Security Technical Implementation Guides (http://iase.disa.mil/stigs/), and National Security Agency Security Configuration Guides. Guidance will be applied to each Air Force information technology system and enclave to establish and maintain a minimum baseline security configuration and posture in accordance with this Instruction and Air Force Instruction 17-101.

7.1.8.   Configuration changes to Air Force information technology CIs must be analyzed and approved by the cognizant configuration and cybersecurity authorities prior to implementation in a production environment. **(T-2)**. Both approved and rejected changes will be formally documented in meeting minutes, and posted in each systems' Risk Management Framework authorization package in accordance with the requirements in Air Force Instruction 17-101.

8.   *Vulnerability Management*

8.1.   A vulnerability management plan consistent with the Cyber Ready 365 initiative must be developed and implemented.

9.   *Incident Response*

9.1.   Plans, processes and standards for reacting to cybersecurity incidents must be developed, approved, and promulgated. The following requirements apply:

9.1.1.   Local standards must be developed to define system events or patterns of events that may be classified as an incident.

9.1.2.   Incident response plans and procedures must be developed for each Air Force system or enclave that define the incident management, handling, and reporting chain, response procedures, and escalation procedures for incidents that develop into a system continuity event. Plans must be exercised/tested on no less than an annual basis.

9.1.3.   Performance records and lessons-learned must be memorialized and retained following exercise/test evolutions.

9.1.4.   Back-ups of critical software and data files must be regularly conducted, maintained, protected, and periodically tested in accordance with Attachment 15, Air Force Incident Response.

9.2.   Systems must be configured to allow users to create content only at their own sensitivity/security level, and view content only at or below their own sensitivity/security level. Spillages (i.e., creation or posting of information at a higher sensitivity/security level than the Air Force information technology is accredited to process, store, or transmit), must be immediately reported in accordance with local procedures, measures taken to prevent the spread of the spillage, and prompt action to clear or sanitize the effected hardware and software. Refer to Air Force Manual 17-1301 for additional guidance.

10. Authorized Use of Personally-owned Devices

10.1.   Personally-owned electronic device users must sign an acceptable use agreement before use in unclassified or classified Air Force spaces.

10.2.   Personally-owned electronic devices (if approved), must obtain Authorizing Official approval prior in order to receive, process, and transmit Department of Defense information, or to operate on or with Air Force Information Technology.

10.3.   Use of personally-owned electronic devices is permitted primarily to facilitate the conduct of government/Air Force business. Limited personal use may be allowed in accordance with local command policies and standards, however, authorized users who are determined to be abusing personal-use privileges will have their access rights suspended or removed.

10.4.   Personally-owned electronic devices connections to the Air Force segment of the Non-Secure Internet Protocol Network, must be encrypted using Air Force-approved software, e.g., Virtual Private Network security software, in accordance with Department of Defense Directive 8100.01 and Department of Defense Instruction 8520.03.

10.5.   Air Force Information Network-connected devices, including personally-owned electronic devices, are subject to monitoring for compliance with applicable policies and standards in accordance with Department of Defense Instruction 8530.01 and Air Force Instruction 17-712.

10.6.   Personally-owned electronic devices that are capable of processing, storing, displaying or transmitting information are prohibited from being introduced into any space where classified information is processed, stored, displayed, discussed, or transmitted, except as noted in the subsections below.

10.6.1. Allowed devices include hearing aids, pacemakers and other implanted medical devices, or personal life support systems. Exercise trackers may be permitted at the discretion of the senior officer in each classified facility/suite.

10.6.2. Disallowed devices include unclassified government cell phones and all personally-owned laptops, tablets, cell phones, pagers, Global Positioning System transceivers, smart watches, music players, wireless keyboards and pointing devices, wireless headphones, and printers. Such devices must be secured outside of classified spaces.

10.6.3. Where secure storage is not available outside of classified spaces, devices with cellular and wireless transmit capabilities may be brought into a classified work space, but must be disabled or powered down prior to entry in accordance with local policy.

10.7. Personally-owned electronic devices are permitted in Air Force spaces where unclassified and/or sensitive information is processed, stored, displayed, discussed, or transmitted. Approved devices include: desktops, laptops, tablets, cell phones, Wi-Fi enabled music players, wireless keyboards and pointing devices, wireless headphones, printers, exercise trackers, pagers, Global Positioning System receivers, hearing aids, pacemakers and other implanted medical devices, or personal life support systems. Such devices may be used subject to the following restrictions; personally-owned electronic devices must:

10.7.1. Be on the list of approved devices. At minimum, they must be commercially obtained in the U.S. or through a U.S. military exchange, and assigned a Federal Communication Commission Identifier denoting compliance with the limits for a Class B digital device designated by the Federal Communication Commission, pursuant to Part 15 of the *Federal Communication Commission Rules*, per Federal Communications Commission Office of Engineering and Technology Bulletin Number 62, *Understanding the Federal Communication Commission Regulations for Computers and Other Digital Devices*.

10.7.2. Control access to information and capabilities with the strongest available mechanism where such capability exists; examples include 2-factor authentication, or a strong password, or a Personal Identification Number of at least six characters.

10.7.3. Have installed only whitelisted applications and receive only updates that do not add any prohibited features or capabilities.

10.7.4. Partition Air Force and other government data from personal data, where such capability exists.

10.7.5. Have up-to-date anti-malware software installed, where such capabilities exist.

10.7.6. Be surrendered to Air Force cybersecurity staff periodically for compliance monitoring when requested.

11. *Authorized use of the internet.* Government-provided hardware and software are for official use and limited authorized personal use only. Limited personal use must be of reasonable duration and frequency that have been approved by the supervisors and do not adversely affect performance of official duties, overburden systems or reflect adversely on the Air Force or the DOD.

11.1. All personal use must be consistent with the requirements of DOD 5500.7-R, Joint Ethics Regulation.

11.2. Internet-based capabilities are all publicly accessible information capabilities and applications available across the Internet in locations not owned, operated, or controlled by the Department of Defense or the Federal Government. Internet-based capabilities include collaborative tools such as SNS, social media, user-generated content, social software, e-mail, instant messaging, and discussion forums (e.g., YouTube, Facebook, MySpace, Twitter, Google Apps).

11.2.1. When accessing Internet-based capabilities using Federal Government resources in an authorized personal or unofficial capacity, individuals shall comply with OPSEC guidance (AFI 10-701, Operations Security) and shall not represent the policies or official position of the Air Force or DOD.

11.3. Examples of authorized limited personal use include, but are not limited to:

11.3.1. Notifying family members of official transportation or schedule changes.

11.3.2. Using government systems to exchange important and time-sensitive information with a spouse or other family members (i.e., scheduling doctor, automobile, or home repair appointments, brief Internet searches, or sending directions to visiting relatives).

11.3.3. Educating or enhancing the professional skills of employees, (i.e., use of communication systems, work-related application training, etc.).

11.3.4. Sending messages on behalf of a chartered organization, (i.e., organizational Booster Club, Base Top 3, Base Company Grade Officers Association, etc.).

11.3.5. Limited use by deployed or TDY members for morale, health, and welfare purposes.

11.3.6. Job searching.

11.4. Inappropriate Use. Using the Internet for other than official or authorized use may result in adverse administrative or disciplinary action. The activities listed in paragraphs 11.4.1. through 11.4.13. involving the use of government-provided computer hardware or software are specifically prohibited. **Failure to observe the prohibitions and mandatory provisions of paragraphs 11.4.1. through 11.4.13 by military personnel is a violation of the Uniform Code of Military Justice (UCMJ), Article 92, Failure to Obey Order or Regulation. Violations by ANG military personnel may subject members to prosecution under their respective State Military Code or result in administrative disciplinary action without regard to otherwise applicable criminal or civil sanctions for violations of related laws. Violations by civilian employees may result in administrative disciplinary action without regard to otherwise applicable criminal or civil sanctions for violations of related laws. Violations by contactor personnel will be handled according to local laws and the terms of the contract.**

11.4.1. Use of Federal government communications systems for unauthorized personal use. See DOD 5500.7-R, *Joint Ethics Regulation (JER)*.

11.4.2. Uses that would adversely reflect on the DOD or the Air Force such as chain letters, unofficial soliciting, or selling except on authorized Internet-based capabilities established for such use.

11.4.3. Unauthorized storing, processing, displaying, sending, or otherwise transmitting prohibited content. Prohibited content includes: pornography, sexually explicit or sexually oriented material, nudity, hate speech or ridicule of others on the bases of protected class (e.g., race, creed, religion, color, age, sex, disability, national origin), gambling, illegal weapons, militancy/extremist activities, terrorist activities, use for personal gain, and any other content or activities that are illegal or inappropriate.

11.4.4. Storing or processing classified information on any system not approved for classified processing.

11.4.5. Using copyrighted material in violation of the rights of the owner of the copyrights. Consult with the servicing Staff Judge Advocate for "fair use" advice.

11.4.6. Unauthorized use of the account or identity of another person or organization.

11.4.7. Viewing, changing, damaging, deleting, or blocking access to another user's files or communications without appropriate authorization or permission.

11.4.8. Attempting to circumvent or defeat security or modifying security systems without prior authorization or permission (such as for legitimate system testing or security research).

11.4.9. Obtaining, installing, copying, storing, or using software in violation of the appropriate vendor's license agreement.

11.4.10. Permitting an unauthorized individual access to a government-owned or government-operated system.

11.4.11. Modifying or altering the network operating system or system configuration without first obtaining written permission from the administrator of that system.

11.4.12. Copying and posting of For Official Use Only, Controlled Unclassified Information, Critical Information, and/or Personally Identifiable Information on DoD–owned, –operated, or –controlled publically accessible sites or on commercial Internet-based capabilities.

11.4.13. Downloading and installing freeware/shareware or any other software product without Authorizing Official approval.

11.5. Official Use, Authorized Use, and Use of Internet-Based Capabilities. Official use of Internet-based capabilities unrelated to public affairs is permitted. However, because these interactions take place in a public venue, personnel acting in their official capacity shall maintain liaison with their public affairs and operations security staff to ensure organizational awareness. Use of Internet-based capabilities for official purposes shall:

11.5.1. Comply with guidance in AFI 10-701, *Operations Security*, AFI 33-322, *Records Management*, AFI 33-364, *Records Disposition-Procedures and Responsibilities*, AFI 33-332, *Privacy Act Program*, and AFMAN 33-363, *Management of Records*.

11.5.2. Be consistent with the requirements of DoD 5500.7-R, *Joint Ethics Regulation (JER)*.

11.5.3. Comply with public affairs Internet-based capabilities guidance.

11.5.4. Ensure that the information posted is relevant and accurate and provide no information not approved for public release, including Personally Identifiable Information.

11.5.5. Provide links to official Air Force content hosted Air Force-owned, -operated, or – controlled sites where applicable.

11.5.6. Include a disclaimer when personal opinions are expressed (e.g., ―This statement is my own and does not constitute an endorsement by or opinion of the Air Force or the Department of Defense‖).

11.5.7. Air Force personnel may subscribe to official government-sponsored news, mail lists, and discussion groups. Some of these products are managed and approved by SAF/PA and accessible from the Air Force Link (http://www.af.mil). Using non-government subscription services without prior approval is misuse of a government system. Subscription or participation in subscription services will be in support of official duties only.

11.6. Managing Web Content. Information systems provide the capability to quickly and efficiently disseminate information. Web content must be managed in compliance with all information management policies and procedures including AFMAN 37-104, *Managing Information to Support the Air Force Mission*.

11.6.1. All DOD telecommunications systems and information systems are subject to monitoring for authorized purposes as prescribed by AFI 33-200, *Information Assurance (IA) Management* and AFI 10-712, *Telecommunications Monitoring and Assessment Program (TMAP)*. Prominently display the exact notice and consent banner specified in AFI 10-712, *Telecommunications Monitoring and Assessment Program (TMAP)* on the first page of all private/intranet web homepages. Notice and consent requirements do not apply to publicly accessible web sites/pages.

11.6.2. The publication of web content available to the public must comply with AFI 35-107, *Public Web Communications* and AFI 35-102, *Security and Policy Review Process* in addition to the official use policies in this section.

12. Mobile Devices

12.1. Mobile computing devices are IS devices such as Portable Electronic Devices, laptops, and other handheld devices that can store data locally and access Air Force-managed networks through mobile access capabilities.

12.2.   All authorized wireless mobile device users will sign the standardized Air Force Form 4433, *US Air Force Unclassified Wireless Mobile Device User Agreement*, and adhere to guidance contained within the agreement when using a wireless mobile computing device. The Air Force Form 4433 is not required for mobile computing devices issued with wireless capabilities disabled.

12.3.   Encrypt all Controlled Unclassified Information transmitted through a commercial or wireless network (e.g., mobile hotspot, commercial Internet café) using an encrypted Virtual Private Network connection or other authorized encryption solution whenever practical. Contact the Enterprise Service Desk or contact the cognizant base Communications Focal Point for installation and usage instructions.

12.4.   Do not operate unclassified wireless technology, devices or services (used for storing, processing, and/or transmitting information), in areas where classified information is discussed, electronically stored, electronically processed, or electronically transmitted without approval of the organizational Information System Security Officer. See Air Force Manual 33-282, *Computer Security* for additional guidance.

12.5.   Only use approved classified wireless devices to store, process, or transmit classified information.

12.6.   Systems and networks must be capable of being configured to disconnect network-connected devices after a defined idle period, or upon violation of a defined system security policy (e.g., attempt to exceed role authority, too many failed login attempts, insertion/connection of a prohibited peripheral device such as a thumb drive)

12.7.   Lost or stolen government mobile computing devices must be reported immediately to your Information System Security Officer.

12.8.   Complete additional Portable Electronic Device and removable storage media training at the organization's discretion here: http://iase.disa.mil/eta/pedrm_v2/pedrm_v2/launchPage.htm.

12.9.   Do not alter or remove any pre-installed software/configurations on end user devices without contacting the Information System Security Officer.

13. Collaborative Computing

13.1.   Collaborative computing (video teleconferencing, etc.) provides an opportunity for a group of individuals and/or organizations to share and relay information in such a way that cultivates team review and interaction in the accomplishment of duties and attainment of mission accomplishment. Contact the Information System Security Officer for guidance on connecting video cameras and microphones to Air Force Information Technology.

14. Public Computing Facilities.

14.1. Air Force Information Technology may not be used in or connected to public computing information systems (Internet cafés and kiosks, hotel business centers, etc.) for processing government-owned unclassified, Controlled Unclassified Information or classified information. Public computing information systems include any information technology resources not under your private or the United States Government's control.

14.2. Using these resources to access web-based government services (e.g., webmail) constitutes a compromise of log-in credentials and must be reported to your Information System Security Officer.

14.3. Connection of privately owned or United States Government controlled mobile computing devices to public networks is permitted to remotely access government services (e.g., webmail) if mobile computing device encryption and connection policies are followed. Public networks include internet service providers for private residences.

15. Malware

15.1. Anti-malware and spam controls must be implemented and continuously updated to protect all Air Force information technology in accordance with Department of Defense Instruction 8500.01 and Air Force Manual 17-1301; organizations owning or operating devices that connect to systems that are not capable of integrating/supporting anti-malware protections must ensure that these devices are provisioned with malware protections that are regularly updated.

16. Specialized Cybersecurity Publications

16.1. Obtaining Cryptologic and Cyber Systems Division publications:

16.1.1. Order Air Force communications security publications through the Communications Material Control System.

16.1.2. Obtain Limited Maintenance Manuals by emailing a request to CCSD/HNC-PSLT at LMM@us.af.mil. Unclassified Methods and Procedures Technical Orders are maintained in the Enhanced Technical Information Management System.

16.2. Accessing Air Force Systems Security Instruction Publications.

16.2.1. Air Force Systems Security Instructions are no longer created or updated and the relevant content is transitioning into Air Force Manuals or Methods and Procedures Technical Orders, if required.

16.2.2. For Official Use Only communications security Air Force Systems Security Instructions are strictly controlled and only available to Communications Security Management System account holders at https://cs3.eis.af.mil/sites/OO-SC-CA-11/default.aspx.

16.2.3. Classified Communications Security Air Force Systems Security Instructions are available upon request by sending an email via the SECRET Internet Protocol Router Network to Air Force Space Command CYSS at usaf.scott.afspc-cyss.mbx.af-comsec-field-support@mail.smil.mil.

16.2.4. Unclassified TEMPEST and Ports, Protocols and Services Management Air Force Systems Security Instructions are located on the Air Force Information Assurance Collaborative Environment SharePoint site at https://cs2.eis.af.mil/sites/10060/Publications/Forms/AllItems.aspx.

Questions regarding this policy can be forwarded to the SAF/CIO A6 Cybersecurity Division, usaf.pentagon.saf-cio-a6.mbx.a6sc-workflow@mail.mil. This Memorandum becomes void after one-year has elapsed from the date of this Memorandum, or upon publication of an Interim Change or rewrite of the affected publication, whichever is earlier.

BRADFORD J. SHWEDO, Lt Gen, USAF
Chief of Information Dominance and
Chief Information Officer

BY ORDER OF THE
SECRETARY OF THE AIR FORCE

AIR FORCE INSTRUCTION 33-200

31 AUGUST 2015
Certified Current 16 February 2016
Communications and Information

COMPLIANCE WITH THIS PUBLICATION IS MANDATORY

ACCESSIBILITY: Publications and forms are available on the e-Publishing website at
www.e-publishing.af.mil for downloading or ordering.

RELEASABILITY: There are no releasability restrictions on this publication.

OPR: SAF CIO/A6SC	Certified by: SAF/CIO A6S (Col Mary Hanson, AF SISO)
Supersedes: AFI 33-200, 23 December 2008; AFI 33-220, 21 November 2007	Pages: 50

This Air Force Instruction (AFI) implements Air Force Policy Directive (AFPD) 33-2, *Information Assurance (IA) Program*, and establishes Air Force (AF) cybersecurity requirements for compliance with: Committee on National Security Systems Instruction (CNSSI) No. 4005, (FOUO) *Safeguarding Communications Security(COMSEC) Facilities and Materials*; Committee on National Security Systems Instruction (CNSSI) No. 4016, (FOUO), *National Policy Governing the Acquisition of Information Assurance (IA) and IA-Enabled Information Technology (IT) Products, CNSSP -11*; Department of Defense (DoD) Chief Information Officer (CIO) Memorandum, *Commercial Mobile Device (CMD) Interim Policy*; DoD Directive (DoDD) 8100.2, *Use of Commercial Wireless Devices, Services and Technologies in the Department of Defense (DoD) Global Information Grid (GIG)*; DoD Instruction (DoDI) 5205.13, *Defense Industrial Base (DIB) Cyber Security/Information Assurance (CS/IA) Activities*; DoDI 8500.01, *Cybersecurity*; DoDI 8510.01, *Risk Management Framework (RMF) for DoD Information Technology (IT)*; DoDI 8420.01, *Commercial Wireless Local-Area Network (WLAN) Devices, Systems, and Technologies*; DoDI 8520.02, *Public Key Infrastructure (PKI) and Public Key (PK) Enabling*; DoDI 8540.01. *Cross Domain (CD) Policy*; DoDI 8520.03, *Identity Authentication for Information Systems*; DoDI O-8530.2, *Support to Computer Network Defense (CND)*; DoDI 8551.01, *Ports, Protocols, and Services Management (PPSM)*; DoDI 8580.1, *Information Assurance (IA) in the Defense Acquisition System*; DoDI 8581.01, *Information Assurance (IA) Policy for Space Systems Used by the Department of Defense*; and DoDI 8582.01, *Security of Unclassified DoD Information on Non-DoD Information Systems*. This instruction is consistent with Chairman Joint Chiefs of Staff Instruction CJCSI 6510.01F, *Information Assurance (IA) and Computer Network Defense (CND)*; CJCSI 6211.02D, *Defense Information Systems network (DISN) Responsibilities* and; Chairman Joint Chiefs of Staff

Manual (CJCSM) 6510.01A, *Information Assurance (IA) and Computer Network Defense (CND) Volume 1 (Incident Handling Program)*. This instruction applies to all AF military, civilian, and contractor personnel under contract by DoD, regardless of Air Force Specialty Code (AFSC), who develop, acquire, deliver, use, operate, or manage AF Information Technology (IT). This instruction applies to the Air National Guard (ANG) and Air Force Reserve Command (AFRC). The term major command (MAJCOM), when used in this publication, includes field operating agencies (FOA) and direct reporting units (DRU). Use of extracts from this instruction is encouraged. CNSSI 4009, *National Information Assurance (IA) Glossary*, explains other terms. Direct questions, comments, recommended changes, or conflicts to this publication through command channels using the AF Form 847, *Recommendation for Change of Publication*, to SAF/CIO A6. Send any supplements to this publication to SAF/CIO A6 for review, coordination, and approval prior to publication. Unless otherwise noted, the SAF/CIO A6 is the waivering authority to policies contained in this publication. The authorities to waive wing/unit level requirements in this publication are identified with a Tier ("T-0, T-1, T-2, T-3") number following the compliance statement. See AFI 33-360, *Publications and Forms Management*, Table 1.1 for a description of the authorities associated with the Tier numbers. Submit requests for waivers through the chain of command to the appropriate Tier waiver approval authority, or alternately, to the Publication OPR for non-tiered compliance items. Ensure that all records created as a result of processes prescribed in this publication are maintained in accordance with (IAW) AFMAN 33-363, *Management of Records*, and disposed of IAW Air Force Records Disposition Schedule (RDS) located in the Air Force Records Information Management System (AFRIMS). The use of the name or mark of any specific manufacturer, commercial product, commodity, or service in this publication does not imply endorsement by the Air Force.

SUMMARY OF CHANGES

This document is substantially changed and should be reviewed in its entirety. The change is a result of a DoD policy directive update and establishes the AF Cybersecurity program and risk management framework as an essential element to accomplishing the AF mission.

Chapter 1

GENERAL INFORMATION

1.1. Introduction. This AFI provides general direction for implementation of cybersecurity and management of cybersecurity programs according to AFPD 33-2. Compliance ensures appropriate measures are taken to ensure the confidentiality, integrity, and availability (CIA) of AF IT and the information they process. This AFI ensures the use of appropriate levels of protection against threats and vulnerabilities, helps prevent denial of service, corruption and compromise of information, and potential fraud, waste, and abuse of government resources.

1.1.1. The AF cybersecurity program incorporates strategy, policy, awareness/training, assessment, authorization, implementation and remediation.

1.1.2. The cybersecurity discipline aligns with the AF Cybersecurity strategy key concept that total risk avoidance is not practical and therefore risks assessment and management is required.

1.1.3. Cybersecurity encompasses the following disciplines/functions: Air Force Risk Management Framework (RMF), IT controls/countermeasures, Communications Security (COMSEC), Computer Security (COMPUSEC), TEMPEST (formerly known as Emissions Security [EMSEC]), AF Assessment and Authorization (A&A) (formerly known as Certification and Accreditation Program [AFCAP]), and Cybersecurity Workforce Improvement Program (WIP).

1.2. Applicability. This publication is binding on all military, civilian and contractors or other persons through the contract or other legally binding agreement with the Department of the Air Force, who develop, acquire, deliver, use, operate, or manage AF IT. This publication applies to all AF IT used to process, store, display, transmit, or protect AF information, regardless of classification or sensitivity. AF IT includes but is not limited to: Information Systems (Major applications & Enclaves), Platform Information Technology (PIT) & PIT systems, IT Services (Internal & External), and IT Products (Software, Hardware, Applications).

1.2.1. More restrictive Federal, DoD, and Director of National Intelligence (DNI) directive requirements governing Special Access Program (SAP) information take precedence over this publication. The latest version of all publications (e.g., Federal, Joint, DoD, AF) referenced within this publication are to be used.

1.2.2. This publication and implementation guidance identified within is not applicable to Intelligence Community ISs to include Sensitive Compartmented Information (SCI) ISs. Refer to the Intelligence Community (IC) Directive (ICD) 503, Intelligence Community Information Technology Systems Security Risk Management, Certification and Accreditation and or the Unified Cross Domain Services Management Office (UCDSMO) as applicable.

1.2.3. Authority for AF space systems rests with Air Force Space Command (AFSPC) as delegated by US Strategic Command (USSTRATCOM). AF space systems generally follow AF Cybersecurity policy and processes; where exceptions exist, this instruction is annotated accordingly. NOTE: Non-AF space systems follow cybersecurity policy and guidance in DoDI 8581.01, Information Assurance (IA) Policy for Space Systems Used by the Department of Defense.

1.2.4. Effective implementation and resultant residual risk associated with cybersecurity controls is assessed, documented, and mitigated according to DoDI 8510.01, DoD Risk Management Framework (RMF), Air Force Manual (AFMAN) 33-210, Air Force Assessment and Authorization Program, and the AF RMF Knowledge Service, for inclusion in the AF Information Technology (IT) A&A package.

1.3. Objectives. The objective of the AF Cybersecurity Program is to manage the risk presented by adversary cyber capabilities (purposeful attacks) and intelligence, environmental disruptions, human or machine errors, and to maintain mission survivability under adversary offensive cyber operations. The AF implements and maintains the Cybersecurity Program to adequately secure its information and IT assets. The Cybersecurity Program:

1.3.1. Ensures AF IT operate securely by protecting and maintaining IS / PIT resources and information processed throughout the system's life cycle.

1.3.2. Protects information commensurate with the level of risk and magnitude of harm resulting from loss, misuse, unauthorized access, or modification.

1.3.3. Leverages the multi-tiered organization-wide risk management approach defined in NATIONAL Institute of Standards and technology (NIST) Special Publication (SP) 800-39, Managing Information Security Risk (See figure 1.1).

1.3.3.1. Tier 1 – Organization: Risk management at this tier is performed through cybersecurity governance bodies at the AF enterprise level.

1.3.3.2. Tier 2 – Mission/Business Process: risk management at this tier is performed by mission owner level and is informed by the risk context, risk decisions, and risk activities at Tier 1.

1.3.3.3. Tier 3 – Information System: risk management at this tier is performed by individuals responsible for the management of individual IT and is guided by the risk context, risk decisions and risk activities at Tiers 1 and 2.

Figure 1.1. Tiered Risk Management Approach (NIST SP 800-39).

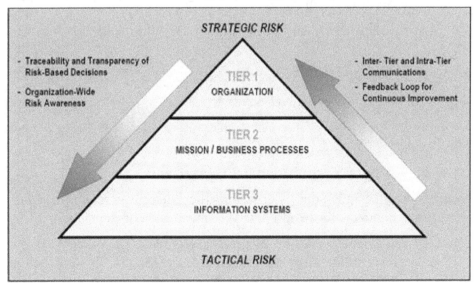

Chapter 2

ROLES AND RESPONSIBILITIES

2.1. Secretary of the Air Force, Office of Information Dominance and Chief Information Officer (SAF/CIO A6) will develop strategies, policy and programs to integrate warfighting and combat support capabilities according to DoDI 8500. 01 and AFPD 33-2. SAF/CIO A6 will:

2.1.1. Oversee the establishment of risk tolerance and baseline cybersecurity controls for the AF IT. SAF CIO A6 will provide guidance to organizations on how to implement solutions for operational requirements exceeding the established National, DoD, Joint Chiefs of Staff (JCS), AF baseline cybersecurity controls for IT and remain within established risk tolerance levels

2.1.2. Maintain visibility of assessment and authorization status of AF IT through automated assessment and authorization tools or designated repositories for the AF in support of DoD CIO and Principle Authorizing Officials (PAO) IAW DoDI 8500.01, Cybersecurity.

2.1.3. Provide guidance to organizations on how to implement solutions for operational requirements exceeding the established National, DoD, Joint Chiefs of Staff (JCS), AF baseline cybersecurity controls for IT and remain within established risk tolerance levels.

2.1.4. Define cybersecurity performance measures and metrics to identify enterprise-wide cybersecurity trends and status of mitigation efforts.

2.1.5. On behalf of the SECAF, and IAW AFPD 33-2, appoint all Authorizing Officials (AO).

2.1.6. Appoint an Air Force Senior Information Security Officer (SISO) to direct and oversee the Air Force Cybersecurity Program.

2.1.7. IAW AFI 33-401, Air Force Architecting, appoint the AF Chief Architect with responsibility for the AF Cybersecurity Architecture.

2.1.8. Serve as the Mission Area Owner (MAO) for the Enterprise Information Environment Mission Area (EIEMA).

2.1.9. Chair the Air Force AO Summit.

2.1.10. Represent the EIEMA in the Air Force AO Summit.

2.1.11. Provide AF Enterprise oversight of the Air Force Information Technology Asset Management (ITAM) program.

2.2. Assistant Secretary of the Air Force (Acquisition) (SAF/AQ) will:

2.2.1. Build cybersecurity into all acquisitions by ensuring all cybersecurity requirements are implemented in all phases and contracts for research, development, test, and evaluation of IT.

2.2.2. Provide streamlined guidance to enable Program Executive Officers (PEO) and Program Managers (PM) to adhere to the mandated standards outlined in this instruction, DoDI 8580.1, DoDI 8581.1, DoDI 8510.01, AFMAN 33-152, and the A&A requirements of AFMAN 33-210.

2.2.3. Ensure contracts include appropriate Defense Federal Acquisition Regulation Supplement (DFARS) clauses for safeguarding unclassified DoD information on non-DoD ISs IAW DoDI 8582.01 and DFARS 204.7304 as applicable.

2.2.4. For all space acquisitions, ensure cybersecurity requirements are implemented in all phases of acquisitions according to the provisions in DoDI 5000.02, Operation of the Defense Acquisition System. SAF/AQ will provide streamlined guidance to enable each program and system under its span of control to develop a cybersecurity strategy meeting the requirements of this instruction, DoDI 5000.02, and DoDI 8580.1, and AFMAN 33-407, Air Force Clinger-Cohen Act (CCA) Compliance Guide.

2.2.5. Manage the process for preparing and reviewing AF acquisition program strategies and ensure cybersecurity has been appropriately addressed.

2.2.6. Represent the AF on policy and procedural matters regarding cybersecurity in the acquisition system.

2.2.7. Coordinate with USAF/A2 to ensure Intelligence acquisition programs address cybersecurity life cycle requirements. SAF/AQ will coordinate with USAF/A2 assigning AF PM representatives for Intelligence systems, equipment, networks, or services on the Air Force Information Network (AFIN) or utilizing AFIN capabilities that were developed and/or acquired by non-AF entities.

2.3. Air Force Office of Special Investigations (AFOSI) will:

2.3.1. AFOSI is the office of primary responsibility (OPR) for on-hook telephone technical security matters, to include providing guidance for installing and operating telephone systems within the Air Force, and department of defense facilities occupied by Air Force personnel.

2.3.2. Provide Air Force representation to the U.S. Government intelligence community's National Telephone Security Working Group (NTSWG). **(T-0)**. The group is the primary technical and policy resource in the U.S. intelligence community for all aspect of the Technical Surveillance Countermeasures (TSCM) program involving telephone systems in areas where sensitive government information is discussed.

2.3.3. Examine the TSCM needs of the Air Force and tailor Air Force telephone security standards to those established by the NTSWG. **(T-0)**.

2.3.4. Provide guidance to Air Force organization on selecting local equipment for installing telephone systems in sensitive discussion areas in conjunction with the host base Communications and Information Systems Officer (CSO) (AFMAN 33-145, Collaboration Services and Voice Systems Management) in accordance with CNSSI No. 5006, National Instruction for Approved Telephone Equipment, and The Defense Information Systems Agency (DISA) Approved Products List Integrated Tracking System (UC system acquisition). **(T-0)**.

2.3.5. Determine the effectiveness and applicability of protective security devices and TSCM procedures for qualified facilities; when warranted provide technical threat information and briefings concerning telephone systems and the countermeasures intended to nullify existing threats. **(T-0)**. Further information on requesting TSCM services or threat briefing is contained in AFI 71-101, Volume 3, The Air Force Technical Surveillance Countermeasures Program.

2.4. Mission Area Owner (MAO). A MAO is appointed for the Air Force portion of each of the DoD MAs. MAOs will:

2.4.1. Oversee and establish direction for the strategic implementation of cybersecurity and risk management within their MAs. **(T-0)**.

2.4.2. Assist the SAF/CIO A6 and the AF SISO in assessing the effectiveness of AF cybersecurity. **(T-1)**.

2.4.3. Coordinate with the DoD PAO for cybersecurity and risk management within their MAs. **(T-0)**.

2.4.4. Represent the interest of the MA, as defined in Reference DoDD 8115.01, Information Technology Portfolio Management, and, as required issue authorization guidance specific to the MA, consistent with this instruction. **(T-0)**.

2.4.5. Resolve authorization issues within their respective MAs and work with other MAOs to resolve issues among MAs, as needed. **(T-0)**.

2.4.6. Nominate AOs for MA IS and PIT systems supporting MA COIs specified in Reference DoD 8320.02, in coordination with SAF/CIO A6, consistent with this instruction. **(T-1)**. SAF/CIO A6 will appoint those nominated by the MAO.

2.4.7. Designate information security architects or IS security engineers for MA segments (overlapping spans of influence (enclaves)) or systems of systems, as needed. **(T-1)**.

2.4.8. Work with the AF SISO and other MAOs to ensure cybersecurity checks and balances occur through the appropriate mission area governance boards. **(T-1)**.

2.5. Twenty-Fourth Air Force (24AF (AFCYBER)) will:

2.5.1. Serve as the single point of contact for processing and supporting AF cybersecurity-related intelligence requests from AF and DoD intelligence entities (e.g., threat assessment against the AFIN) for the AFIN. 24 AF (AFCYBER) will provide SAF/CIO A6 Staff with courtesy copies of requests and responses for assessment of impact on the AF cybersecurity Program.

2.5.2. Coordinate with Joint and Defense-wide program offices to ensure interoperability of cybersecurity solutions across the DODIN.

2.5.3. Provide support to national, DoD, and AF level Technical Advisory Groups (TAG) (i.e., AFIA TAG, RMF TAG, DoD PPS TAG, etc.), as requested by SAF/CIO A6.

2.5.4. Oversee, manage, and control AF enclave boundary defense activities, measures, and operations.

2.5.5. Issue time compliance technical orders and modification kits for cybersecurity and cybersecurity-enabled products or components of AF ITs.

2.5.6. Ensure Ports Protocols and Services (PPS) requirements for the AFIN are limited to only those required for official use with proper approval, PPS's not properly approved follow the deny by default, allow by exception access philosophy, and that PPS information is validated annually.

2.6. AF Senior Information Security Officer (SISO) will develop, implement, maintain, and enforce the AF Cybersecurity Program. The AF SISO will direct and coordinate any associated budgets and advocate for AF-wide cybersecurity solutions through the planning, programming, budget and execution process on behalf of the SAF/CIO A6 according to DoDI 8500.01, DoDI 8510.01, AFPD 33-2, and AFMAN 33-210. The SISO is referred to as Senior Agency Information Security Officer [SAISO] or Chief Information Security Officer [CISO] in CNSSI 4009. The AF SISO will:

2.6.1. Be a DoD official (O-6 or GS-15 at a minimum), and a United States citizen.

2.6.2. Complete training and maintain cybersecurity certifications IAW AFMAN 33-285, Cybersecurity Workforce Improvement Program.

2.6.3. Monitor, evaluate, and provide advice to the SAF/CIO A6 regarding AF cybersecurity posture.

2.6.4. Serve as the AF CIO's primary liaison to DoD SISO, Component SISO's, MAJCOM Cybersecurity Offices, AF AOs, and SCAs.

2.6.5. In coordination with the SAF/CIO A6 and AO's, ensure cybersecurity risk posture and risk tolerance decisions for AF IT meet mission and business needs while also minimizing the operations and maintenance burden on the organization. The AF SISO will represent the AF at Federal, DoD, and Joint cybersecurity steering groups and forums.

2.6.6. Ensure that IT guidelines are incorporated into acquisition, implementation, and operations and maintenance functions.

2.6.7. Provide direction on how cybersecurity metrics are determined, established, defined, collected, and reported for compliance with statutory, DoD, Joint, and AF policies and directives.

2.6.8. Appoint Security Control Assessors (SCAs) for all AF IT (excluding Special-Access Program/Special Access Required [SAP/SAR], IC, Space, NC3, and Medical).

2.6.9. Perform as the SCA or formally delegate the security control assessment role for governed information technologies.

2.6.10. Provide guidance and direction on Agent of the Security Control Assessor (ASCA) establishment in support of Assessment and Authorization (A&A) requirements.

2.6.11. Oversee establishment and enforcement of the A&A process, roles, and responsibilities; review approval thresholds and milestones within the AF A&A Program.

2.6.12. Chair the Air Force Cybersecurity Risk Management Council (AFCRMC).

2.6.13. Adjudicate IT determinations, in coordination with the Air Force Risk Management Council, when there is a conflict in the IT determination process.

2.6.14. Appoint in writing the AF Certified TEMPEST Technical Authority (AF CTTA).

2.6.15. Appoint AF members to the DoD RMF TAG.

2.6.16. Review and approve Cybersecurity Strategies for all AF IT IAW DoDI 5000.02 and AFMAN 33-407, AF Clinger-Cohen Act (CCA) Compliance Guide. The approval of the Cybersecurity Strategies cannot be delegated.

2.6.17. Review and approve Privacy Impact Assessments (PIAs) submitted IAW AFI 33-332, The AF privacy and Civil Liberties Program. The approval of the PIA may be not be delegated.

2.6.18. Approve National Security System (NSS) designations for AF IT.

2.6.19. Approve Defense Industrial Base Cybersecurity/Information Assurance (DIB/CS/IA) Damage Assessment Reports (as needed) IAW DoDI 5205.13.

2.6.20. Ensure AF RMF guidance is posted to the DoD Component portion of the KS, and is consistent with DoD policy and guidance.

2.6.21. Validate and prioritize (with the support of the AF Risk Management Council (AFRMC)) all AF cryptographic certification requests prior to submission for NSA action.

2.7. Air Force Office of Cyberspace Strategy and Policy (SAF CIO A6S) will:

2.7.1. Provide cyberspace policy, guidance, & oversight. SAF CIO A6S will inform Headquarters United States Air Force, and MAJCOMs about changes to DoD and AF cybersecurity policies and procedures in accordance with HAFMD1-26 Chief, Information Dominance and Chief Information Officer.

2.7.2. Ensure AF acquisition guidance reflects national, federal, DoD, and AF cybersecurity policy and procedures.

2.7.3. Develop and evaluate cybersecurity performance measurements for compliance with statutory, DoD, Joint, and AF policies and directives.

2.7.4. Establish and enforce the RMF process, roles, and responsibilities; review approval thresholds and milestones within the AF RMF Program.

2.7.5. Provide AF IT PEO's guidance on completion and submission of Cybersecurity Strategies and submit for AF SISO approval.

2.7.6. Collect and report cybersecurity management, financial, and readiness data to meet DoD cybersecurity and Office of Management and Budget (OMB) reporting requirements.

2.7.7. Serve as the single cybersecurity coordination point for joint or Defense-wide programs that are deploying IT (guest systems) to AF enclaves.

2.7.8. Participate in Federal, DoD and Joint cybersecurity and RMF technical working groups and forums (e.g. RMF TAG, DSAWG).

2.7.9. Develop and implement AF cybersecurity requirements planning, programming, budgeting, and execution in the AF budget process in compliance with SISO direction. Through the Air Force budget request, SAF CIO A6S will advocate for cybersecurity funding and manning with the Office of the Secretary of Defense and Congress.

2.7.10. Establish and maintain cybersecurity checklists for use with the AF Inspection Systems, currently the Management Internal Control Toolset (MICT) in accordance with AFI 90-201 Air Force Inspection System.

2.7.11. Develop concepts and establish strategy for integrated support and configuration management of cybersecurity equipment.

2.7.12. Oversee, plan, implement, manage, and support the COMSEC aspects of programs, including centralized record maintenance of COMSEC equipment, components, and material.

2.7.13. Carry out Federal Information Security Management Act of 2002 (FISMA)-related CIO responsibilities.

2.7.14. Provide detailed information on the FISMA requirements via the annual AF FISMA Reporting Guidance.

2.7.15. Manage the annual assessment of the AF Cybersecurity Programs as required by FISMA. Requests, through channels, support from AF organizations. Organizational support allows the AF SISO to answer the annual FISMA report questions posed by the OMB.

2.7.16. Ensure cybersecurity requirements are addressed and visible in all investment portfolios and investment programs according to AFI 33-401, Air Force Architecting, and AFMAN 33-210

2.7.17. Implement and enforce the education, training, and certification of AF cybersecurity professionals and users according to DoD 8570.01-M, Information Assurance (IA) Training, Certification, and Workforce Management, and AFMAN 33-285.

2.7.18. Coordinate Inspector General (IG) inspections and associated responsibilities according to and AFI 90-201.

2.7.19. Collect and report on qualification metrics and submits reports to the DoD CIO as directed such as for Federal Information Security Management Act (FISMA) reporting, standardizing reporting across Air Force.

2.7.20. Review and provide guidance in support of MAJCOM or equivalent provided commercial internet waivers and facilitates presentation to the DoDIN waiver panel; is a voting member of the DoDIN waiver panel. For additional information, AFI 33-115 and AFMAN 33-282.

2.7.21. Review Cross Domain Solution (CDS) requests and presents to the Defense Security Accreditation Working Group (DSAWG) for approval.

2.7.22. Manage the implementation of policy and standardized procedures to catalog, regulate, and control the use and management of ports, protocols, and services (PPS) in IT and applications IAW DoDI 8551.01.

2.7.23. Serve as the AF Public Key Infrastructure (PKI Management Authority (PMA). SAF CIO A6S will direct policy, requirements, and implementation of PKI integration across all AF networks. SAF CIO A6S will participate in DoD and Federal working groups and forums involved in PKI and IdAM, and is the AF OPR to DoD, NSS, and Federal PKI and Identity and Access Management (IdAM) groups.

2.7.24. Represent the AF as a voting member on DoD PPS Configuration Control Boards (CCB). Designates AF A6S as primary and one or more alternate voting representatives for the DoD PPS CCB.

2.7.25. Designate a primary and one or more alternate representatives for the DoD PPS TAG.

2.7.26. Designate points of contact to register the PPS used by AF IS in the DoD PPS Registry (also known as DoD PPS Database) according to this instruction and DoD policy.

2.7.27. Manage PPS procedures for the AF according to this instruction, DoD guidance, and USCYBERCOM orders and directives. Responsibilities include advocating issues from customers with Air Staff and the DoD PPS Program Manager at the Defense Information Systems Agency (DISA); providing guidance and support to customers; and processing waiver, deviations, and exceptions.

2.7.28. Establish a Defense Industrial Base Cyber Security/ Information Assurance (DIB CS/IA) Program Office. The DIB CS/IA Program Office works cooperatively with participating Cleared Defense Contractors (CDCs) to enhance their ability to safeguard DoD information residing on or transiting DIB unclassified networks IAW DoDI 5205.13, Defense Industrial Base Cyber Security/Information Assurance Activities. In accordance with DoDI 5205.13, the AF established the AF Damage Assessment Management Office (AF DAMO) within SAF/CIO A6.

2.7.29. The AF DAMO will conduct damage assessments on data compromised as a result of adversary intrusions into those contractor networks. AF DAMO determines the extent of intelligence obtained by adversary cyber intrusions into DIB networks, and assesses the overall impact of the data loss on current and future weapons programs, scientific and research projects, and warfighting capabilities.

2.7.30. Set policy for managing AF electronic (EM) spectrum use to support the AF mission and exercise control over the frequency management process IAW AFI 33-580, Spectrum Management

2.7.31. Upon request from the AF SISO, AF functional authorities and MAJCOMs are required to provide appropriate programmatic, operational, and technical SMEs, intelligence analysts, or cyber forces to assess the compromised information as part of Integrated Process Teams (IPTs). All IPTs convene at the DoD Cyber Crime Center (DC3) in Linthicum, MD, where AF DAMO personnel assist the IPT in the damage assessment process. The participants provide expert opinion on the extent of damage caused as a result of the compromise and make recommendations on mitigation efforts required due to the loss of that information. Damage assessment reports are drafted for each case and disseminated to the appropriate AF program offices, agencies, and stakeholders for review and possible mitigation actions.

2.8. Authorizing Official (AO). The AO is the official with the authority to formally assume responsibility for operating a system at an acceptable level of risk. The AO renders authorization decisions for DoD ISs and PIT systems under their purview in accordance with DoDI 8510.01. A current listing of AOs is available on the AF Cybersecurity Knowledge Service located at: **https://cs1.eis.af.mil/sites/SAFCIOA6/A6S/afcks/Compliance/AFAAP/SitePages/Home.aspx**. The AO will:

2.8.1. Be appointed from senior leadership positions within business owner and mission owner organizations to promote accountability in authorization decisions that balance mission and business needs and security concerns/risks.

2.8.2. Be a DoD official (O-7 or SES at a minimum), and be a United States citizen.

2.8.3. Complete AF AO training IAW AFMAN 33-285.

2.8.4. Be appointed by SAF CIO/A6 in coordination with the appropriate MAO. The appointment grants authority to authorize IS and PIT systems within the authorization boundary as needed.

2.8.5. Not delegate ATO granting authority. **(T-1)**.

2.8.6. For additional information on this position, see AFMAN 33-210, Air Force Assessment and Authorization Program.

2.9. AO Designated Representative (AODR) will:

2.9.1. Complete AO training and maintain cybersecurity certifications consistent with duties and responsibilities of an SCA and IAW AFMAN 33-285. **(T-1)**.

2.9.2. Perform responsibilities as assigned by the AO. NOTE: AODR's may perform any and all duties of an AO except for accepting risk by issuing an authorization decision. **(T-1)**.

2.9.3. Make recommendations to the AO to approve ATO based on input from RMF team members, and other AOs and AODRs. **(T-1)**.

2.9.4. Be appointed by the AO, and, at a minimum, be an O-5 or GS-14. **(T-1)**.

2.10. Security Control Assessor (SCA).

2.10.1. The SCA is the senior official having the authority and responsibility for the certification of all ISs and PIT systems governed by the Air Force.

2.10.2. For additional information on this position, see AFMAN 33-210, Air Force Assessment and Authorization Program.

2.11. Security Controls Assessor Representative (SCAR) will:

2.11.1. Complete training and maintain appropriate cybersecurity certification IAW AFMAN 33-285. It is highly recommended SCARs complete both the AO training module and attain the CNSSI 4016 certificate for supplemental training. Proof of training (e.g. certificate) is included as an artifact to the IS's or PIT system's A&A package.

2.11.2. For additional information on this position, see AFMAN 33-210, Air Force Assessment and Authorization Program

2.12. Agent of the Security Controls Assessor (ASCA). The ASCA is a licensed organization which may be contracted by the PM to assist in certification activities and will:

2.12.1. Report directly to the SCA for guidance related to validation activities and procedures. **(T-1)**.

2.12.2. Maintain ASCA license IAW SISO guidance and the ASCA licensing guide. **(T-1)**.

2.12.3. For additional information on this position, see AFMAN 33-210, Air Force Assessment and Authorization Program

2.13. Information System Owners (ISO). Official responsible for the overall procurement, development, integration, modification, or operation and maintenance of an information or PIT system. An ISO will be appointed in writing for every IS and PIT System. **(T-1)**. For those systems that are Air Force-wide systems (e.g., AFNET, LOGMOD, etc.), they will be appointed by the HAF/SAF 3-letter responsible for the capability. For MAJCOM, base-level IS/PIT systems, and base enclaves, the appropriate MAJCOM 2-letter will appoint the ISO. No further appointment is necessary. The ISO will:

2.13.1. Identify the requirement for IT and requests funds, operates and maintains the IT in order to enhance mission effectiveness. (NOTE: Do not confuse this with the ISO role in TEMPEST.) **(T-2)**.

2.13.2. Identify, implement, and ensure full integration of cybersecurity into all phases of their acquisition, upgrade, or modification programs, including initial design, development, testing, fielding, operation, and sustainment. **(T-0)**. Reference DoDI 8510.01, AFI 63-101, and AFMAN 33-210 for guidance.

2.13.3. Develop, maintain, and track the security plan for assigned IS and PIT systems. **(T-1)**.

2.13.4. Develop and document a system-level continuous monitoring (CM) strategy to monitor the effectiveness of security controls employed within or inherited by the system, and monitoring of any proposed or actual changes to the system and its environment of operation. **(T-1)**. The ISO must ensure the strategy includes the plan for annual assessments of a subset of implemented security controls, and the level of independence required of the assessor (e.g., SCA or ASCA). **(T-1)**.

2.13.5. Ensure the PMO is resourced with individuals knowledgeable in all areas of cybersecurity to support security engineering and security technical assessments of the IS or PIT systems for the SCA's authorization determination, AOs authorization decision, and other security related assessments (e.g., Financial Improvement and Audit Readiness (FIAR) IT testing, Inspector General audits). (T-1).

2.13.6. Ensure that applicable CTO's are received and acted upon per the CTO directions. **(T-1)**.

2.13.7. Ensure stakeholders are identified that may be affected by the implementation and operation of the IT. **(T-2)**.

2.13.8. Ensure the IT has a designated Information System Security Manager (ISSM) with the support, authority, and resources to satisfy established responsibilities for managing the IT's cybersecurity posture. **(T-1)**.

2.13.9. Plan and budget for all software assurance (SwA) activities (e.g. adopt SwA best practices, third party, secure coding standards, automated scans, etc…) during all phases of the software development lifecycle (SDLC). **(T-2)**.

2.13.10. In coordination with the Information Owner/Steward, decide who has access to the system (and with what types of privileges or access rights) and ensure system users and support personnel receive the requisite security training (e.g., instruction in rules of behavior). **(T-2)**.

2.13.11. Based on guidance from the SCA and AO, inform appropriate organizational officials of the need to conduct the full RMF assessment and authorization; ensure the necessary resources are available for the effort, and provides the required IT access, information, and documentation to the SCA. **(T-2)**.

2.13.12. Receive the security assessment results from the SCA and develop a POA&M for all identified weaknesses. **(T-1).** After taking appropriate steps to reduce or eliminate weaknesses, the ISO will assemble the authorization package and submit the package to the SCA for assessment and subsequently to the AO for an authorization decision. **(T-1).**

2.13.13. Ensure open POA&M items are closed on time. **(T-2).**

2.13.14. Ensure consolidated A&A documentation is maintained for systems with instances at multiple locations. **(T-2).**

2.13.15. Ensure, with the assistance of the ISSM, the system is deployed and operated according to the approved System Security Plan (SSP) and the authorization package (i.e., the AO's authorization decision). **(T-1).**

2.13.16. Conduct specific duties outlined in the KS. **(T-2).**

2.14. Program Manager (PM)/System Manager (SM). PM/SMs will:

2.14.1. Identify, implement, and ensure full integration of cybersecurity into all phases of their acquisition, upgrade, or modification programs, including initial design, development, testing, fielding, operation, and sustainment IAW AFI 63-101, Acquisition and Sustainment Life Cycle Management, DoDI 8510.01 and AFMAN 33-210 for guidance. **(T-0).**

2.14.2. Plan and coordinate for all IT cybersecurity requirements IAW applicable guidance. **(T-2).**

2.14.3. Ensure that ISs and PIT systems under their purview have cybersecurity-related positions assigned in accordance with AFMAN 33-285. **(T-2).**

2.14.4. Assign an ISSM for the program office and ensure they have the proper certification IAW AFMAN 33-285. **(T-1).**

2.14.5. Ensure the IS or PIT system is registered IAW AFI 33-141, AF IT Portfolio Management and Investment Review.

2.14.6. Develop and maintain a cybersecurity strategy as applicable and IAW AFMAN 33-407.

2.14.7. Ensure operational systems maintain a current ATO. **(T-1).**

2.14.8. Ensure all changes are approved through a configuration management process, are assessed for cybersecurity impacts and reported to the SCA as applicable. **(T-2).**

2.14.9. Track and implement the corrective actions identified in the POA&M in the Enterprise Mission Assurance Support Service (eMASS). **(T-0).** POA&Ms provide visibility and status of security weaknesses to the ISO, Information Owner(s), AO and AF SISO.

2.14.10. Ensure annual and milestone security reviews are conducted and selected RMF controls are tested IAW this instruction, the CM plan and OMB Circular A-130, Management of Federal Information Resources ISO FISMA. **(T-0).** The PM/SM will brief the results of both security reviews and the RMF control tests at the governance boards for the appropriate mission area in accordance with the board requirements. **(T-0).**

2.14.11. Report security incidents to stakeholder organizations. **(T-2).** The PM/SM will conduct root cause analysis for incidents and develop corrective action plans. **(T-2).**

2.14.12. Ensure the program is resourced with individuals knowledgeable in security engineering and security technical assessments IAW AFMAN 33-285. **(T-2)**. These efforts support the SCA's assessment and the AO's authorization decision for IT that is subject to the RMF process IAW AFMAN 33-210.

2.14.13. In coordination with the Information Owner/Steward, ensure that a Privacy Impact Assessment is completed for IT that process and/or stores Personal Identifiable Information (PII). **(T-0)**.

2.15. Information System Security Manager (ISSM). The ISSM is the primary cybersecurity technical advisor to the AO for AF IT. For base enclaves, the ISSM manages the installation cybersecurity program, typically as a function of the Wing Cybersecurity Office. That program ISSM may also serve as system ISSM for the enclave and reports to the CS/CC as the PM for the base enclave. The ISSM will:

2.15.1. Act on behalf of the AO to maintain the authorization of the system throughout its lifecycle; therefore, if the ISSM is not qualified to serve, the AO or the AODR may request the PM/SM designate a suitable replacement. **(T-3)**.

2.15.2. Complete training and maintains cybersecurity certification IAW AFMAN 33-285 (Individuals in this position must be US citizens). **(T-0)**. Proof of training (e.g. certificate) is included as an artifact to the IS's or PIT systems A&A package.

2.15.3. Support the ISO on behalf of the AO in implementing the RMF. **(T-3)**.

2.15.4. For additional information on this position, see AFMAN 33-210, Air Force Assessment and Authorization Program.

2.16. Information System Security Officer (ISSO). The ISSO is responsible for ensuring the appropriate operational security posture is maintained for AF IT under their purview. This includes the following activities related to maintaining situational awareness and initiating actions to improve or restore cybersecurity posture. ISSOs (formerly system level IA Officers), or the ISSM if no ISSO is appointed, will:

2.16.1. Implement and enforce all AF cybersecurity policies, procedures, and countermeasures using the guidance within this instruction and applicable cybersecurity publications. **(T-1)**.

2.16.2. Complete and maintain required cybersecurity professional certification IAW AFMAN 33-285 (Individuals in this position must be US citizens). **(T-0)**.

2.16.3. For additional information on this position, see AFMAN 33-210, Air Force Assessment and Authorization Program.

2.17. Cybersecurity Liaison. Each organizational command or other cognizant authority (i.e., group commander, Wing Cybersecurity Office) must appoint a Cybersecurity Liaison (formerly Organizational IAO) when cybersecurity functions are consolidated to a central location or activity. **(T-1)**. Additional (subordinate) cybersecurity liaison positions may be assigned for additional support at the discretion of organizations or based upon mission requirements, however, only one primary and one alternate cybersecurity liaison is mandatory. A cybersecurity liaison will:

2.17.1. Develop, implement, oversee, and maintain an organization cybersecurity program that identifies cybersecurity requirements, personnel, processes, and procedures. **(T-1)**.

2.17.2. Supervise the organization's cybersecurity program. **(T-2)**.

2.17.3. Implement and enforce all Air Force cybersecurity policies and procedures using the guidance within this instruction and applicable specialized (COMSEC, COMPUSEC, TEMPEST etc.) cybersecurity publications. **(T-1)**.

2.17.4. Assist the wing cybersecurity office in meeting their duties and responsibilities. **(T-3)**.

2.17.5. Ensure all users have the requisite security clearances, supervisory need-to-know authorization, and are aware of their cybersecurity (via cybersecurity training) before being granted access to Air Force IT according to AFMAN 33-282, chapter 4, AFI 31-501 and AFMAN 33-152. **(T-1)**.

2.17.6. Ensure all users receive cybersecurity refresher training on an annual basis. **(T-2)**.

2.17.7. Ensure IT is acquired, documented, operated, used, maintained, and disposed of properly and in accordance with the IT's security A&A documentation as prescribed by AFMAN 33-210. **(T-1)**.

2.17.8. Ensure proper CM procedures are followed. **(T-1)**. Prior to implementation and contingent upon necessary approval according to this instruction and AFMAN 33-210, the cybersecurity liaison will coordinate any changes or modifications to hardware, software, or firmware with the wing cybersecurity office and system-level ISSM or ISSO. **(T-1)**.

2.17.9. Report cybersecurity incidents or vulnerabilities to the wing cybersecurity office. **(T-3)**.

2.17.10. In coordination with the wing cybersecurity office, initiate protective or corrective measures when a cybersecurity incident or vulnerability is discovered. **(T-3)**.

2.17.11. Implement and maintain required cybersecurity (COMSEC, COMPUSEC and TEMPEST) countermeasures and compliance measures IAW AFI 10-712, Telecommunications Monitoring and Assessment Program (TMAP). **(T-1)**.

2.17.12. Initiate requests for temporary and permanent exceptions, deviations, or waivers to cybersecurity requirements or criteria according to this instruction and applicable specialized cybersecurity publications. **(T-1)**.

2.17.13. When called upon to assist with an assessment conducted by the DIB CS/Cybersecurity program office, provide subject matter experts to analyze the data and provide recommendations for further action. **(T-3)**.

2.17.14. Maintain all IS authorized user access control documentation IAW the applicable Air Force records Information Management System (AFRIMS). **(T-3)**.

2.18. Information Systems Security Engineer (ISSE). The ISSE is any individual, group, or organization responsible for conducting information system security engineering activities. Reference NIST SP 800-37, *Applying the Risk Management Framework to Federal Information Systems*, for additional details.

2.18.1. Information system security engineering is a process that captures and refines information security requirements and ensures that the requirements are effectively integrated into information technology component products and information systems through purposeful security architecting, design, development, and configuration.

2.18.2. Information system security engineers are an integral part of the development team (e.g., integrated project team) designing and developing organizational information systems or upgrading legacy systems.

2.18.3. Information system security engineers employ best practices when implementing security controls within an information system including software engineering methodologies, system/security engineering principles, secure design, secure architecture, and secure coding techniques.

2.18.4. System security engineers coordinate their security-related activities with information security architects, senior information security officers, information system owners, common control providers, and information system security officers.

2.18.5. IAW DoD 8570.01-M, Personnel performing any IA Workforce System Architecture and Engineering (IASAE) specialty function(s) (one or more functions) at any level must be certified to the highest level function(s) performed. **(T-0)**.

2.19. Information Owner/Steward. An organizational official with statutory, management, or operational authority for specified information and the responsibility for establishing the policies and procedures governing its generation, collection, processing, dissemination, and disposal as defined in CNSSI 4009, National Information Assurance Glossary. The Information Owner/Steward will:

2.19.1. Plan and budget for security control implementation, assessment, and sustainment throughout the system life cycle, including timely and effective configuration and vulnerability management. **(T-2)**.

2.19.2. Establish the rules for appropriate use and protection of the subject information (e.g., rules of behavior) and retain that responsibility even when the information is shared with or provided to other organizations. **(T-1)**.

2.19.3. Provide input to ISOs on the security controls selection and on the derived security requirements for the systems where the information is processed, stored, or transmitted. (A single IS may contain information from multiple information owners/stewards.) **(T-1)**.

2.19.4. Where a single IS may contain information from multiple information owners/stewards, provide input to ISO for the IS regarding security controls selection and derived security requirements for the systems where the information is processed, stored, or transmitted. **(T-1)**.

2.19.5. Thoroughly review the assessment and then releases the authorization package to the AO, thereby indicating to the AO that the system's cybersecurity posture satisfactorily supports mission, business, and budgetary needs (i.e., indicates the mission risk is acceptable); enabling the AO to balance mission risk with community risk in an authorization decision. **(T-1)**.

2.19.6. Maintain statutory or operational authority for specified information and responsibility for establishing the controls for its generation, collection, processing, dissemination, and disposal. **(T-0).**

2.20. Headquarters Air Force Space Command (HQ AFSPC). As Lead Command for all Air Force Cyberspace Operations via the 24AF(AFCYBER), AFSPC is the Air Force focal point for establishment, operation, maintenance, defense, exploitation, and attack Cyberspace Operations. AFSPC coordinates the prioritization of all Cyberspace Infrastructure requirements. AFSPC will:

2.20.1. Cyber orders issued by AFSPC/CC or his/her delegated representative are military orders issued by order of the Secretary of the Air Force.

2.20.2. Support PEOs and PMs in the research, development, test and evaluation, and sustainment of cybersecurity or cybersecurity-enabled capabilities of AF space systems and products in consultation with the other MAJCOMs.

2.20.3. Develop and sustain processes for rapid cybersecurity capability insertion to address new or rapidly developing threats to the AFIN.

2.20.4. Ensure space PEOs and PMs/ISOs comply with cybersecurity requirements outlined in DoDI 8580.1, DoDI 8581.01, this instruction, and AFMAN 33-210.

2.20.5. Establish cybersecurity education and training for space PEOs and PMs/ISOs according to the requirements outlined in AFMAN 33-285.

2.20.6. Manage and advise the CDS program for space systems.

2.20.7. Manage the AF Cryptologic Modernization Program and oversees the AF COMSEC Office of Record (CoR) for COMSEC IAW AFMAN 33-283.

2.20.8. Coordinate all cryptographic equipment requests to reduce duplication of effort and ensure sustainability.

2.20.9. Manage all requests for support from NSA for cryptographic equipment certification, coordinate validation, and recommend prioritization for the AF SISO

2.20.10. Perform responsibilities IAW AFMAN 33-286, Air Force TEMPEST Program. This includes developing/managing necessary forms to include the AF Form 4170, Emission Security Assessments/Emission Security Countermeasures Review. AFSPC will executes the TEMPEST program and coordinates with the AF CTTA, as outlined in AFSSI 7700 (to become AFMAN 33-286).

2.20.11. Establish and maintain Method and Procedure Technical Orders (MPTOs) associated with cybersecurity policies.

2.20.12. Implement the AF cybersecurity workforce certification and training program according to DoDD 8570.01, DoD 8570.01-M, and AFMAN 33-285.

2.20.13. Review, evaluate, and interpret AF cybersecurity doctrine, policy, and procedures. AFSPC will make recommendations on implementation of the doctrine, policy, and procedures to SAF/CIO A6.

2.20.14. Develop, coordinate, promulgate, and maintain AF (component-level) cybersecurity control specifications applicable to ISs residing on or connecting to the AFIN, if required.

2.20.15. Provide guidance and support to cybersecurity offices in developing, implementing, and managing their cybersecurity programs.

2.20.16. Establish a Cross Domain Solution Office (CDSO) to manage the AF CDS program.

2.20.17. Advocate issues from customers with Air Staff and the CDS Secret Internet Protocol Router Network Connection Approval Office at DISA.

2.20.18. Serve as the AF focal point for coalition networking issues specific to the command, control, communications and computers infrastructure, core e-mail, file sharing, print, collaboration tools, video teleconferencing (VTC), and web browsing capabilities. AFSPC will coordinate with focal points of other functional communities (AF/A2, etc.) on coalition networking issues for other infrastructures (intelligence, surveillance, and reconnaissance, etc.).

2.20.19. Provide the following to SAF CIO/A6 and the SISO:

2.20.19.1. Situational awareness (SA) report on the operational status and network health of the globally interconnected, end-to-end set of AF unique information capabilities, and associated processes for collecting, processing, storing, disseminating, and managing information on-demand to warfighters, policy makers, and support personnel, including owned and leased communications and computing systems and services, software (including applications), mission, SPO and PMO managed systems and enclaves, data, and security.

2.20.19.2. SA report related to outage and other network events impacting the AFIN or the supported Combatant Command (COCOM) mission.

2.20.19.3. SA report on completion of cyber orders or inability to complete assigned tasks.

2.20.19.4. Tasks specified above do not replace any requirement for OPREP reporting outlined in AFI 10-206.

2.20.20. Manage the AF PPS program and procedures according to this instruction, DoDI 8551.01, and USCYBERCOM orders. Advocate issues from customers with AF/A3C/A6C Staff and the DoD PPS Program Manager at DISA.

2.20.21. Advocate issues from AF activities with DoD PPS Management.

2.20.22. Provide guidance and support regarding PPS policy and procedures.

2.20.23. Serve as the primary with one or more alternate AF representatives to the DoD PPS TAG according to DoD guidance.

2.20.24. Serve as the primary POC with one or more alternates to register (aka declare) and maintain PPS for AF ISs in the DoD PPS central Registry according to DoD 8551.01.

2.20.25. Support and manage the AF PKI Systems Program Office (PKI SPO) to manage AF identity credentials for human and non-person entities. AFSPC will provide guidance and support to that office in the implementation and management of PKI and other IdAM capabilities to support Air Force operational and mission needs.

2.20.26. Process requested for PPS exceptions, deviations, or waivers according to this instruction and DoD policy and guidance (e.g. DoD 8551.01, USCYBERCOM orders, PPSM Exception Management Process).

2.20.27. Execute the AF COMSEC program and perform COMSEC responsibilities IAW AFMAN 33-283, Communications Security (COMSEC) Operations.

2.20.28. Perform responsibilities IAW AFMAN 33-286. This includes developing/managing necessary forms to include AF Form 4170, Emission Security Assessments/Emission Security Countermeasures Reviews.

2.21. MAJCOM Cybersecurity Office or Function will:

2.21.1. Support the principles of availability, integrity, confidentiality, authentication, and non-repudiation of information and information systems for the purpose of protecting and defending the operation and management of Air Force IT and National Security System (NSS) assets and operations.

2.21.2. Develop implement, oversee, and maintain a MAJCOM cybersecurity program that identifies cybersecurity architecture; requirements; objectives and policies; personnel; and processes and procedures.

2.21.3. Ensure cybersecurity workforce is identified, trained, certified, qualified, tracked, and managed IAW DoD and AF cybersecurity Workforce Improvement Program (WIP) directives and policies such as DoDD 8570.01, DoD 8570.01-M, AFMAN 33-210 and AFMAN 33-285. NOTE: If the individual is performing only COMSEC management duties, DoD 8570.01-M does not require the individual to be certified under this program.

2.21.4. Report the status of their cybersecurity workforce (civilian, military, and contractors) qualifications to the SAF/CIO A6 IAW Paragraph 7.2.of AFMAN 33-285.

2.21.5. Ensure that AF PKI Local Registration Authorities (LRAs) are established and maintained at all MAJCOM bases

2.21.6. Serve as a member of any appropriate Configuration Control Boards (CCB) or steering groups to address MAJCOM cybersecurity program issues.

2.21.7. Coordinate Inspector General (IG) inspections and associated responsibilities according to and AFI 90-201.

2.21.8. Review AF Form 4169 exception/waiver submissions, as appropriate, to maintain situational awareness

2.21.9. Ensure proper identification of manpower and personnel assigned to cybersecurity functions. MAJCOM Cybersecurity Office/Function will ensure this information is entered and maintained in the appropriate Air Force personnel databases.

2.21.10. IAW AFI 10-712, maintain organizational e-mail account with an SMTP alias of <MAJCOM>.cybersecurity@us.af.mil

2.22. Wing Cybersecurity Office (WCO). Develops and maintains the wing cybersecurity program. The wing cybersecurity office addresses all cybersecurity requirements on the base for IT under the control of the base Communications Squadron/Flight, including IT of tenant units (i.e., FOAs, DRUs, and other service units) unless formal agreements exist. NOTE: For bases with more than one wing, the designated host wing is responsible to provide this function. For Joint bases, the AF is responsible for all AF-owned IT and infrastructure. The WCO will:

2.22.1. IAW AFMAN 33-285, track and manage cybersecurity positions assigned by a commander which includes: system ISSMs/ISSOs assigned by PM's, COMSEC Account Managers (CAMs), COMSEC Responsible Officers (CROs), Cybersecurity Liaisons, Privileged Users, and Secure Voice Responsible Officers (SVROs).

2.22.2. Assign trained cybersecurity personnel IAW DoD requirements for IAM Level I or Level II categories and ensure certifications are also maintained IAW DoD requirements. **(T-0)**. *NOTE:* If the individual is performing only COMSEC management duties, refer to AFMAN 33-285 for position specific certifications.

2.22.3. Manage the overall COMSEC posture of their installation. The WCO will appoint one primary and at least one alternate COMSEC manager to oversee the wing COMSEC program and to assist and advise them in COMSEC matters IAW AFMAN 33-283, COMSEC Operations. **(T-0)**. The wing commander may delegate appointment authority to the unit commander of the supporting COMSEC account.

2.22.4. Establish COMPUSEC in the host wing cybersecurity office. **(T-1)**. The cybersecurity office addresses all COMPUSEC requirements on the base, including those of tenant units (i.e. FOAs, DRUs, and other MAJCOM units) unless formal agreements exist.

2.22.5. Establish TEMPEST in the host wing cybersecurity office. **(T-1)**. The cybersecurity office addresses all TEMPEST requirements on the base, including those of tenant units (i.e. FOAs, DRUs, and other MAJCOM units) unless there are other formal agreements.

2.22.6. Manage the Identity Management Program (PKI, Common Access Card (CAC), Air Force Directory Service (AFDS) Programs) IAW AFMAN 33-282.

2.22.7. Assist all base organizations and tenants in the development and management of their cybersecurity program. **(T-1)**.

2.22.8. Designate a base enclave ISSM (for organization-level cybersecurity program) to develop, implement, oversee, and maintain the installation cybersecurity program. **(T-1)**.

2.22.9. Provide oversight and direction to Cybersecurity Liaison (for organizational level programs) according to this instruction, AFI 33-115 and specialized cybersecurity publications. **(T-1)**. Specific responsibilities include but are not limited to the below items. The WCO will:

2.22.9.1. Ensure Cybersecurity Liaison receives proper cybersecurity training. **(T-1)**.

2.22.9.2. Ensure Cybersecurity Liaisons are aware of and follow cybersecurity policy and procedures. **(T-1)**.

2.22.9.3. Ensure Cybersecurity Liaison s review weekly alerts, bulletins, and advisories impacting security of an organization's cybersecurity program. **(T-1)**.

2.22.10. Ensure cybersecurity guidance, and standard operating procedures (SOP) are prepared, maintained, and implemented by each unit. **(T-3)**.

2.22.11. Monitor implementation of cybersecurity guidance and ensure appropriate actions to remedy cybersecurity deficiencies. **(T-3)**.

2.22.12. Ensure cybersecurity inspections, tests, and reviews are coordinated. **(T-3)**.

2.22.13. Ensure all cybersecurity management review items are tracked and reported. **(T-3)**.

2.22.14. Report security violations and incidents to the AO and Air Force network operations activities according to AFI 33-115, Air Force Information Technology (IT) Service Management) and CJCSM 6510.01B, Cyber Incident Handling Program. **(T-1)**.

2.22.15. Ensure cybersecurity incidents are properly reported to the AO and the Air Force network operations reporting chain, as required, and that responses to cybersecurity related alerts are coordinated; all according to the requirements of AFI priveleged115. **(T-1)**.

2.22.16. Ensure software management procedures are developed and implemented according to configuration management (CM) policies and practices for authorizing use of software on ISs. **(T-1)**.

2.22.17. Serve as member of the base-level CM board or delegates this responsibility to an appropriate Action Officer. **(T-3)**.

2.22.18. Maintain organizational e-mail account with an SMTP alias of <wing>.cybersecurity@us.af.mil. **(T-3)**.

2.23. Organizational Commander. Commander will assign one Cybersecurity Liaison and at least one alternate to execute cybersecurity responsibilities protecting and defending information systems by ensuring the availability, integrity, confidentiality, authentication, and non-repudiation of data through the application of cybersecurity measures outlined herein. **(T-1)**. Commanders or equivalent at all levels will maintain these responsibilities through the following programs:

2.23.1. Computer Security (COMPUSEC) Program IAW AFMAN 33-282.

2.23.2. Communications Security (COMSEC) Program IAW AFMAN 33-283.

2.23.3. TEMPEST Program Management IAW AFMAN 33-286. TEMPEST: A name referring to the investigation, study, and control of compromising emanations from telecommunications and automated information systems equipment.

2.23.4. On-Hook Telephone Security Program. **(T-1)**. Organization commanders will ensure their program meets the following:

2.23.4.1. Ensure the number of telephones used is the minimum necessary to meet operational requirements. **(T-3)**.

2.23.4.2. Apply appropriate telephone security measures in discussion areas and ensure adequate protection for classified or sensitive discussions IAW National telephone Security Working group (NTSWG) publications. **(T-3)**.

2.23.4.3. Use physical security safeguards to prevent unauthorized personnel from obtaining clandestine physical access to the telephone system or components of the system. **(T-3)**.

2.24. Privileged User with cybersecurity responsibilities (e. g. Functional System Administrator). NOTE: Enterprise Information System (EIS) content managers and site designers (e.g. Microsoft SharePoint Site Owners, AF Portal Content Managers) who don't have administrative privileges to the overall IS are not considered Privileged Users. Additionally,

AFMAN 33-285 and AFI 33-115 identify those individuals with certain elevated rights who are not considered Privileged users. Privileged users will:

2.24.1. Complete training and maintains certification IAW AFMAN 33-285.

2.24.2. Configure and operate IS according to cybersecurity policies and procedures and notify the AO, ISSM or ISSO of any changes that might adversely impact cybersecurity. **(T-1).**

2.24.3. Ensure IT under their management is properly patched per guidance from the PEO. **(T-3).**

2.24.4. Conduct and document annual cybersecurity inspection of their IT per the guidance provided the IT PEO. **(T-3).** Provides report to WCO annually.

2.24.5. Establish and manage authorized user accounts for ISs, including configuring access controls to enable access to authorized information and removing authorizations when access is no longer needed. **(T-3).**

Chapter 3

CYBERSECURITY GOVERNANCE

3.1. Cybersecurity Governance.   Cybersecurity governance occurs at all levels of the Air Force enterprise and ensures cybersecurity strategies are aligned with mission and business objectives, are consistent with applicable laws and regulations through adherence to policies and internal controls, and provide assignment of responsibility.   The Air Force Cybersecurity Governance Structure (Figure 3.1) formalizes how the AF manages cybersecurity risk with respect to the existing Air Force and DoD corporate boards and processes. The intention is to ensure cybersecurity is addressed in the appropriate forums for both mission/business risk and IT investment/portfolio management.   Current governance forums do not regularly discuss cybersecurity nor the risk management process on a regular basis. These new forums ensure these topics are raised to the appropriate level and informed decisions can be made.

Figure 3.1. Air Force Cybersecurity Governance.

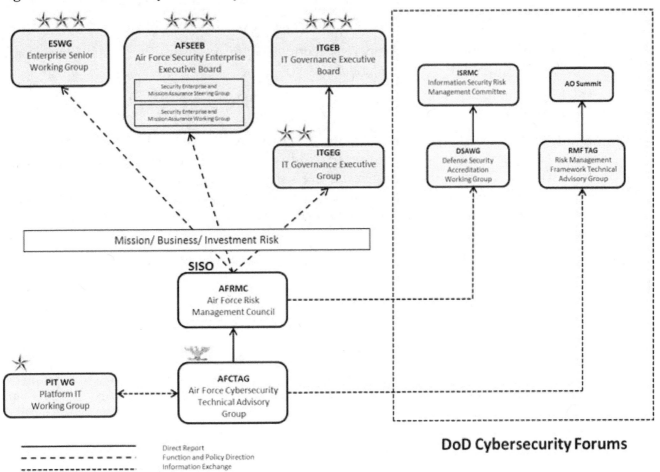

3.2. Governance Process. The governance process ensures compliance with Title 44 United States Code (USC) § 3541, Federal Information System Management Act of 2002 (FISMA), requiring senior agency officials to provide security for information and ISs that support the operations and assets under their control.

3.3. Governance Bodies. The Air Force leverages existing Air Force and DoD governance bodies (shaded areas of Figure 3.1—AFSEEB, ITGEB, ITGEG, ESWG, etc.) to discuss cybersecurity risk topics and make organizational and mission/business area risk decisions. This instruction does not define the scope or responsibilities of these existing bodies. The following governance groups provide focused management and oversight of the Air Force Cybersecurity Program. Charters and process guides for each of these organizations are in development.

3.4. Air Force Risk Management Council (AFRMC). The AFRMC provides a forum for the senior cybersecurity professionals to validate and vet issues concerning cybersecurity risk from a mission and business perspective. The council reviews proposed Mission Area or DoD Component RMF control overlays, A&A guidance, and additional AF controls for compatibility with baseline controls and with other established control sets. They standardize the cybersecurity implementation processes for both the acquisition and lifecycle operations of Air Force Information Technology and Cyberspace systems. They advise and make recommendations as needed to existing governance bodies. Finally, they adjudicate assignment of Air Force Information Technology and Cyberspace systems to the appropriate Authorizing Official for those systems which fall outside of the defined authorization boundaries.

3.4.1. Chaired by the AF Senior Information Security Officer (AF SISO)

3.4.2. Attendees include all Air Force Security Control Assessors, 24 AF/A3, 624 OC, and SAF/CIO A6C Mission Area Integrators (MAI)

3.4.3. Monthly VTC or SIPR Defense Collaboration Services (DCS) with an annual in-person meeting

3.5. AF Cybersecurity Technical Advisory Group (AFCTAG). The AFCTAG provides technical cybersecurity subject matter experts (SMEs) from across the MAJCOMs and functional communities to facilitate the management, oversight, and execution of the AF Cybersecurity Program. The TAG examines cybersecurity related issues common across Air Force entities and provide recommendations to the AF SISO and DSWAG on changes to the baseline security controls or configurations.

3.5.1. Co-chaired by the SAF/CIO A6S Cybersecurity Division Chief and AFSPC/A6S Division Chief

3.5.2. Attendees include all MAJCOM and functional cybersecurity subject matter experts

3.5.3. Quarterly DCS

3.6. AF AO Summit. The AO Summit is not a governance body but rather an enabler for both an enterprise-wide and converged organizational perspective to cybersecurity policy development, oversight, implementation, and training. This venue provides the CIO and Authorizing Officials an opportunity to discuss issues relevant and significant to AOs and their SCAs and develop recommended a way-forward for use by the Department.

3.6.1. Chaired by SAF CIO/A6

3.6.2. Attendees include all Air Force Authorizing Officials, Mission Area Owners (MAO), 24 AF/CC, and AF SISO

3.6.3. Quarterly VTC with an annual in-person meeting

Chapter 4

CYBERSECURITY IMPLEMENTATION

4.1. Air Force Cybersecurity Program. The AF Cybersecurity Program synchronizes and standardizes the cybersecurity requirements of AF IT.

4.1.1. Cybersecurity is integrated into all aspects of the AF Enterprise Architecture according to AFI 33-401.

4.1.2. Cybersecurity professionals coordinate cybersecurity projects across multiple investments through Portfolio Management according to AFI 33-141, Air Force Information Technology Portfolio Management and Investment Review.

4.1.3. All elements of an IT cybersecurity program are developed, documented, implemented, and maintained through the AF A&A program. Please reference AFMAN 33-210 for further information.

4.1.4. Cybersecurity professionals adhere to CJCSI 6510.01F and AFI 33-115 on use of DoD-provided, enterprise-wide automated tools/solutions (e.g., Host Based Security System (HBSS)) to ensure interoperability with DoD- and AF- provided enterprise-wide solutions for remediation of vulnerabilities for endpoint devices.

4.1.5. ISSMs and ISSOs protect ISs, their operating system, peripherals (media and devices), applications, and the information it contains against loss, misuse, unauthorized access, or modification. Ensure compliance with AFMAN 33-282 and MPTO 00-33B-5006, End-point Security for Information Systems. These procedures ensure the computing environment complements the AF IS cybersecurity program. MPTO 00-33B-5006 provides standard procedures derived from cybersecurity controls and other measures for organizations to maintain the confidentiality, integrity, and availability of any AF IS cybersecurity program

4.1.6. All authorized users ensure protection of all ISs against tampering, theft, and loss. Protect ISs from insider and outsider threats by controlling physical access to the facilities and data by implementing procedures identified in Joint, DoD, AF publications, and organizationally created procedures. Basic end point security procedures are located in MPTO 00-33B-5006.

4.2. Cybersecurity Workforce Training and Certification. This instruction and supporting cybersecurity specialized publications standardize the naming conventions and functions of AF organizational (management) and IT level (technical or system-level) Cybersecurity personnel. These documents also prescribe training and certification requirements according to national and DoD policy consistent with and supplementary to the guidance outlined in AFMAN 33-285, Information Assurance (Cybersecurity) Workforce Improvement Program.

4.3. Information Assurance Workforce System Architecture and Engineering. IAW DoD 85701-M and AFMAN 33-285, personnel required to perform any IA Workforce System Architecture and Engineering (IASAE) specialty functions (one or more functions) at any level must be certified to the highest level functions(s) performed. **(T-1).**

4.3.1. Cybersecurity privileged user or management functions, see AFMAN 33-285.

4.3.2. AO and other A&A training requirements, see AFMAN 33-285.

4.3.3. COMPUSEC training and requirements, see AFMAN 33-282

4.3.4. COMSEC training requirements follow guidance in AFMAN 33-283

4.3.5. TEMPEST training requirements, see AFMAN 33-286.

4.4. Cybersecurity Inspections. Cybersecurity disciplines are assessed under the Air Force Inspection System (AFIS) IAW AFI 90-201 and through self-assessments communicators (SACs) located in MICT.

4.4.1. Inspectors/auditors perform inspections according to guidance in this instruction and applicable AF Cybersecurity publications for COMSEC, COMPUSEC, and TEMPEST (Formerly known as EMSEC).

4.4.2. ISOs comply with formal testing and certification activities according to AFI33-210.

4.4.3. Inspect or assess performance measures and metrics based on enterprise-wide (and individual elements where appropriate) cybersecurity performance and assess cybersecurity trends. Limit the measurements and metrics to Federal and DoD Cybersecurity reporting requirements.

4.4.4. Inspect AF PKI Local Registration Authorities (LRAs) in accordance with AFMAN 33-282 and associated MICT section.

4.5. Notice and Consent Monitoring and Certification. All AF installations, AF organizations on joint bases, circuits, and ISs must comply with DoD notice and consent certification requirements for monitoring to occur by authorized activities as well as comply with installation certification procedures IAW AFI 10-712, Telecommunications Monitoring and Assessment Program (TMAP) (to become Cyberspace Defense Analysis (CDA) Operations and Notice and Consent Process). **(T-0).**

4.6. Connection Management.

4.6.1. AF activities must adhere to the DISA Connection Approval Process if the system is connected to the Non-Secure Internet Protocol Router Network (NIPRNET) or Secure Internet Protocol Router Network (SIPRNET). **(T-0).** Connection Approval Process information can be found at **http://www.disa.mil/connect**. For all AF ISs accessing the DISN, get appropriate service (e.g., DISA) coordination and authorization before proceeding with combatant command coordination and/or Joint Staff approval.

4.6.2. AF activities comply with AFMAN 33-210 for connection approval to the Air Force Information Networks (AFIN).

4.6.3. AF A6S provides AF representation to the DSAWG. The DSAWG represents the DISN community and advises the DISN AOs of community acceptance or rejection of risk. DISN connection decisions rest with the DISN AOs. AF A6S work with AF activities involved in the adjudication of conflicts related to DISN connection decisions.

4.7. Commercial Internet Service Providers (ISPs). The only DoD authorized access to the Internet is via a NIPRNET connection.

4.7.1. Organizations requiring a connection (wired or wireless) to the Internet via a fixed Commercial ISP solution must accredit the system and submit an AF Form 4169, Request for Waiver from Cybersecurity Criteria, through their WCO through AFSPC's Cyberspace

Support Squadron (CYSS) to SAF CIO/A6SC, the AF representative to the DoDIN Waiver Panel (GWP) IAW CJCSI 6211.02D. **(T-2)**. Use AF Form 4169 to document the request and prepare a DoDIN waiver brief in accordance with the DISA, "DISN Connection Process Guide" (**http://www.disa.mil/connect/waivers**). This applies to all Commercial ISP connection requests IAW AFI 33-115.

4.7.2. Use of mobile air cards and/or mobile hotspots for Temporary Duty (TDY)/mobile usage does not require a Commercial ISP waiver. Obtain approved devices and mobile data service through IT Commodity Council (ITCC) approved contracts. Use of these devices and services is not to be permanent. Configure all mobile hotspots and devices to applicable DISA Wireless STIGs. Use only approved encryption solutions (e.g. Cisco VPN Client, Juniper Network Connect, Citrix). Refer to DISA STIGs for use of mobile hotspot feature on Commercial Mobile Devices (CMDs)/smartphones. Organizations that use DoD devices that attach to the NIPR via these means must ensure they connect through a VPN first. **(T-2)**. Any other configuration is unauthorized.

4.8. Cross-Domain Solutions (CDS). Cross Domain Solutions (CDS). A CDS is a form of controlled interface providing the ability to manually and/or automatically access and/or transfer information between different security domains (e.g., between unclassified and classified). A CDS requires an additional approval process and authorization, separate from the review and approval for the Authorization to Connect (ATC) for the Command Communications Service Designator (CCSD). Developers and users refer to the CDS guidance, use only CDS-approved devices evaluated and validated through Certification Test and Evaluation or have a sufficient body of evidence to allow the Air Force Cross Domain Support Element (AF CDSE) to conduct a thorough risk analysis and adhere to CDS configuration guidelines. The purpose of and approval procedures for CDS are extracted from DoD, DISA, NSA, and the Unified Cross Domain Systems Management Office (UCDSMO) policies and guidance. For guidance on the most current CDS process, contact the AF CDSE, consult DoDI 8540.01, Cross Domain (CD) Policy, or visit the DISA Mission Partners website at **http://disa.mil/Services/Network-Services/Enterprise-Connections/Mission-Partner-Training-Program**.

4.8.1. Send all requests for CDSs and coalition information sharing solutions to AF CDSE at **nac.csni@us.af.mil** (**https://intelshare.intelink.gov/sites/afcdse/SitePages/Home.aspx**). This office provides the most current guidance for the CDS approval process..

4.8.2. The UCDSMO maintains a baseline list of NSA-certified solutions available for reuse contingent on approval by the DSAWG (available on SIPRNet at **https://intelshare.intelink.sgov.gov/sites/ucdsmo/default1.aspx**)

4.9. Security Configuration Management and Implementation. The ISSO (or designee) will comply with the following:

4.9.1. Securely configure and implement all IT products. **(T-1).** Cybersecurity reference documents, such as NIST SPs, DISA STIGs (**http://iase.disa.mil/stigs/**),NSA Security Configuration Guides, and other relevant publications are used as security configuration and implementation guidance. ISSOs will apply these reference documents according to this policy and AFMAN 33-210 to establish and maintain a minimum baseline security configuration and posture. **(T-1).**

4.9.2. Review all changes to the configuration of IT (i.e., the introduction of new IT, changes in the capability of existing IT, changes to the infrastructure, procedural changes, or changes in the authorized or privileged user base, etc.) for cybersecurity impact prior to implementation. **(T-2)**. Document all configuration management and security requirements in the IT A&A package according to AFMAN 33-210 and CJCSI 6510_01F. **(T-0)**.

4.9.3. NIST Cryptographic Module Validation Program (CMVP) for Federal Information Processing Standard (FIPS) 140-2, Security Requirements for Cryptographic Modules, validation.   **(T-0)**:   **http://csrc.nist.gov/groups/STM/cmvp/documents/140-1/140val-all.htm**

4.9.4. Leverage and update DISA Approved Products List Integrated Tracking System (APLITS). **https://aplits.disa.mil/ (T-1)**

4.10. IT Acquisitions and Procurement.   All acquisition and cybersecurity personnel must ensure cybersecurity is implemented in all IT acquisitions at levels appropriate to the system characteristics and requirements throughout the acquisition life cycle, according to AFI 63-101 and AFMAN 33-153.

4.10.1. All acquisition and cybersecurity personnel must ensure all IT hardware, firmware, and software components or products incorporated into DoDIN comply with evaluation and validation requirements in DoDI 8500.01 and CNSSP 11. **(T-1)**. Refer to CNSSP No. 11 for the latest process and policy guidance on this subject. Limit products to those listed on any of the lists below:

4.10.1.1. NSA-certified   "TEMPEST"   products: **https://www.nsa.gov/applications/ia/tempest/tempestPOCsCertified.cfm**

4.10.1.2. Common   Criteria   Evaluation   and   Validation   Scheme   (CCEVS): **http://www.commoncriteriaportal.org/products** and **http://www.niap-ccevs.org**

4.10.1.3. DoD   Unified   Capabilities   Approve   Products   List   (UC   APL): **https://aplits.disa.mil/**

4.10.1.4. AF   Evaluated   Products   List   (AF   EPL) **https://cs.eis.af.mil/afdaa/Lists/COTSGOTS%20Software/EPL.aspx**

4.10.1.5. Product   Director   Automated   Movement   and   Identification   Solutions ((PDAMIS) @**http://www.pdamis.army.mil**

4.10.2. Cybersecurity and Cybersecurity-enabled products are documented within the IS A&A package according to AFMAN 33-210.

4.10.3. WCOs, ISSOs, and ISSMs must ensure the procurement activities of all IT hardware, cellular, and peripheral devices (e.g., desktops, laptops, servers, BlackBerry® devices, tablets, cell phones, printers, scanners) follow the guidance in AFMAN 33-153, and the AF ITCC guidance available on the AF Portal. **(T-2)**.

4.10.4. WCOs, ISSOs, and ISSMs must ensure the procurement of telephone/voice switches is coordinated with Air Force Office of Special Investigations (AFOSI) for Technical Surveillance Countermeasures (TSCM) program. **(T-1)**.

4.10.5. IAW AFI 71-101, Volume 3, Air Force Technical Surveillance Countermeasure Program, the acquisition of voice systems require certification through the UC APL.

4.11. Air Force KMI. The Air Force Lifecycle Management Center (AFLCMC) manages the Air Force KMI program. KMI is the framework and services that provide the generation, production, storage, protection, distribution, control, tracking and destruction for all cryptographic keying material, symmetric keys as well as public keys and PKI certificates. The KMI system is comprised of nodes that provide the means to deliver cryptographic products, key management products and services to a large and diverse community of globally distributed users. ISOs and Cybersecurity professionals implement key management procedures according to AFMAN 33-283.

4.12. Public Key Infrastructure (PKI). The AF PKI SPO (AFLCMC/HNCYP) is responsible for the integration, implementation and sustainment of the DoD PKI, NSS PKI, AF PKIs, external federated PKIs and associated identity and access control management (ICAM) technologies to deny anonymity to our adversaries within the AF and associated COCOM systems. PKI authenticates users and systems on all AF networks via multiple, interoperable PKIs. PKI digital certificates provide both human identity credentials as well as non-person entity (NPE) identity credentials for all personnel, systems, services, devices, applications and data across all AF networks. ISOs and Cybersecurity professionals implement PKI, ICAM and Identity and Access Management (IdAM) procedures in accordance with AFMAN 33-282.PKI is implemented by AF ISOs and Cybersecurity professionals through the use of hardware tokens (CAC, AFNET-S token, Alternate Login Token (ALT), and Volunteer Logical Access Credential (VoLAC)) and software certificates on both AFNET and AFNET-S according to procedures in AFMAN 33-282.

4.13. System Security Engineering (SSE). Cybersecurity is to be integrated into the overall system acquisition and engineering process throughout the entire system life cycle via the information system's security engineering (SSE), according to DoDI 5134.16, *Deputy Assistant Secretary of Defense for Systems Engineering.*

4.14. COMPUSEC. The framework of the AF COMPUSEC IA program consists of a cyclic sequential security management model for risk management. This model is specific to information processed on AF computing systems and incorporates strategy, policy, awareness/training, implementation, assessment, remediation, and mitigation controls IAW AFMAN 33-283.

4.15. Communications Security. COMSEC refers to measures and controls taken to deny unauthorized persons information derived from ISs of the United States Government related to national security and to ensure the authenticity of such ISs. COMSEC protection results from applying security measures (i.e., crypto security, transmission security, etc.) to communications and ISs generating, handling, storing, processing, or using classified or sensitive government or government-derived information, the loss of which could adversely affect the national security interest. It also includes applying physical security measures to COMSEC information or materials. Ensure all COMSEC activities comply with AFMAN 33-283 and associated AF Cybersecurity publications.

4.16. TEMPEST. TEMPEST denies interception and exploitation of classified, and in some instances unclassified, information by containing compromising emanations within a facility where information is being processed. Refer to AFMAN 33-286 for implementing countermeasures to protect against compromising emanations.

4.17. Operations Security (OPSEC).   The OPSEC program is an operations function or activity and its goals are information superiority and optimal mission effectiveness. The emphasis is on OPERATIONS and the assurance of effective mission accomplishment. To ensure effective implementation across organizational and functional lines the organization's OPSEC Program Manager (PM), Signature Management Officer (SMO), or coordinator resides in the operations and/or plans element of an organization or report directly to the commander. For additional information see AFI 10-701, Operations Security (OPSEC).

4.18. Incident Response and Reporting.   An incident is defined as an assessed occurrence that actually or potentially jeopardizes the confidentiality, integrity, or availability of an IS; or the information the IS processes, stores, or transmits; or that constitutes a violation or imminent threat of violation of security polices, security, procedures, or acceptable use policies (see CNSSI 4009).

4.18.1. For reportable cyber incidents (e.g., unauthorized access, denial of service, and malicious logic) in the AF network response hierarchy, refer to AFI 10-1701.

4.18.2. For any other service incident, which is defined as an unplanned interruption to an IT service or reduction in the quality of an IT service, contact the applicable helpdesk.

4.18.3. For COMPUSEC incidents refer to AFMAN 33-282.

4.18.4. For COMSEC incidents refer to AFMAN 33-283.

4.19. Mobile Code.   Comply with DoDI 8500.01 to protect ISs from the threat of malicious or improper use of mobile code during system acquisition and fielding. System developers and implementers follow guidelines in all applicable STIGs. Additional mobile code guidance is in AFMAN 33-282.

4.20. Ports, Protocols, and Services (PPS).   The AF PPS Management Program provides policy and procedures on the use of PPS across the AFIN, consistent and complementary with the implementation of DoDI 8551.01, Ports, Protocols, and Service Management (PPSM), for additional PPS requirements, see AFSSI 8551, Ports, Protocols, and Services (PPSM) Management.

4.21. Physical Security.   Access to and Physical Protection of Computing Facilities. Employ physical security measures (i.e., access control, visitor control, physical control, testing, etc.) for network and computing facilities that process publicly releasable, sensitive, or classified information to only authorized personnel with appropriate clearances and a need-to-know according to AFJI 31-102, Physical Security and DoD 5200.08-R, Physical Security Program.

4.22. Information Security.   Comply with AFI 16-1404 for workplace security procedures and storage of documents and IT equipment.

4.23. Malicious Logic Protection.   Protect AF IT from malicious logic (e.g., virus, worm, Trojan horse) attacks by applying a mix of human and technological preventative measures according to DoD 8500.01 and AFMAN 33-282. Continuous monitoring and patching of IS and PIT systems are mandated per AFMAN 33-210.

4.24. Data Encryption.   Protect sensitive information; Controlled Unclassified Information (CUI); For Official Use Only (FOUO); Personally Identifiable Information (PII); Health Insurance Portability and Accountability Act (HIPAA); Privacy Act (PA); in transit and at rest with strong encryption, IAW DoD CIO Memorandum, and USCYBERCOM CTO 08-001,

Encryption of Sensitive Unclassified Data at Rest (DaR) on Mobile Computing Devices and Removable Storage Media Used Within the Department of Defense (DoD) and this instruction. For additional encryption requirements see, AFMAN 33-282.

4.25. Mobile Computing Devices. Mobile computing devices are IS devices such as Portable Electronic Devices (PEDs), laptops, and other handheld devices that can store data locally and authenticate to AF-managed networks through mobile access capabilities. Refer to AFMAN 33-282 for additional information on protections, deployment, use of Software Certificates and support of mobile computing devices.

4.26. Personal Activity Monitor (PAM) / Wearable Technology. Any non-stationary electronic apparatus with the capability of detecting, recording, storing, and or transmitting information about an individual's activity level, biological functions, or similar activities related to health and fitness. For additional information refer to AFMAN 33-282.

4.27. Wireless Services. WCOs, ISSOs, and ISSMs must ensure wireless services integrated or connected to AF ISs comply with DoDI 8500.01and DoDD 8100.02, Use of Commercial Wireless Devices, Services, and Technologies in the Department of Defense (DoD) Global Information Grid (GIG). **(T-0).** Refer to AFMAN 33-282 for additional information on protections, deployment and support of wireless services.

4.28. Non-Air Force IT utilized on AF installations.

4.28.1. Privately-owned Hardware and Software. Privately-owned hardware and software connected to the AFIN and used to process unclassified and/or unclassified sensitive information requires operational mission justification and AFIN AO approval. Document the approval between the user and government organization. The organizational ISSO maintains the documentation and provides it to the system ISSM as required. For additional information see AFMAN 33-282.

4.29. Peripheral Devices. A computer peripheral is any external device that provides input and output for the computer. Inputs devices transmit data and/or commands to a desktop or laptop (e.g. mouse, scanners, Smart boards, pointers, and keyboards). Output devices receive data from the desktop or laptop providing a display or printed product (e.g. monitors, printers, and multi-function devices (MFDs)). Refer to AFMAN 33-282 for additional information on the protections for peripheral devices.

4.30. Removable Media. Removable media is any type of storage media designed to be removed from a computer. This includes external hard drives, optical media (e.g., CDs, DVDs) and flash media (e.g., memory cards, USB flash drives, and solid-state drives). Refer to AFMAN 33-282 for additional information on removable media handling, configuration and use.

4.31. Collaborative Computing. Collaborative computing provides an opportunity for a group of individuals and/or organizations to share and relay information in such a way that cultivates team review and interaction in the accomplishment of duties and attainment of mission accomplishment. Configure and control collaborative computing technologies to prevent unauthorized users from seeing and/or hearing national security information and material at another user's workstation area. Establish safeguards to ensure the integration of data from various sources does not result in the creation of a higher classified data on ISs that are not rated to store or process at the higher level. Such instances are considered spillage and WCOs, ISSOs, and ISSMs must address these. **(T-1)**. Refer to AFMAN 33-282 for additional information on collaborative computing and provisions on its deployment and use.

4.32. Spillage.   This is when data is found on a system that has a lower security classification than that of the data. This term is also used when PII is found on a system that is not approved for processing, storing or transmitting of PII data. Refer to AFMAN 33-282, for additional information on spillage and incident reporting.

WILLIAM J. BENDER, Lt Gen, USAF
Chief of Information Dominance and
Chief Information Officer

Attachment 1

GLOSSARY OF REFERENCES AND SUPPORTING INFORMATION

References

Public Law 100-235, *Computer Security Act of 1987*, January 8, 1988

Title 5 USC § 552a, *The Privacy Act of 1974, as amended* January 7, 2011

Title 10 USC § 2224, *Defense Information Assurance Program*, January 7, 2011

Title 44 USC § 3541, *Information Security (Federal Information System Management Act)*, December 17, 2002

Title 44 USC § 3602, *Office of Electronic Government*, December 17, 2002

OMB Circular A-130, *Management of Federal Information Resources*, November 28, 2000

ICD 503, *Intelligence Community Information Technology Systems Security Risk Management, Certification and Accreditation,* September 15, 2008

CNSSP 26, *National Policy on Reducing the Risk of Removable Media for National Security Systems*, November 2010

CNSSI 4009, *National Information Assurance (Cybersecurity) Glossary*, April 26, 2010

CNSSI 4031, *Cryptographic High Value Products*, 16 February 2012

NIST 800-37, Guide for Applying the Risk Management Framework to Federal Information Systems: A Security Life Cycle Approach, Rev 1, February 2010

NIST 800-39, Managing Information Security Risk: Organization, Mission, and Information System View, March 2011

NIST-SP 800-46, *Guide to Enterprise Telework and Remote Access Security,* April 2010

NIST-SP 800-88 Revision 1, *Guidelines for Media Sanitization, December 2014*

National Science and Technology Council Subcommittee on Biometrics Glossary, September 14, 2006

NSTISSAM TEMPEST/2-95A, *Red/Black Installation Guidance*, February 3, 2000

NSTISSI 4003, (FOUO) *Reporting and Evaluating COMSEC Incidents (U)*, December 2, 1991

CNSSI 4005, (FOUO) *Safeguarding Communications Security (COMSEC) Facilities and Materials*, August 22, 2011

CNSSI No. 4016, (FOUO) *National Information Assurance Training Standard For Risk Analysis*

CNSSI 4031, *Cryptographic High Value Products (CHVP)*, February 16, 2012

CNSSP 11, *National Policy Governing the Acquisition of Information Assurance (IA) and IA-Enabled Information Technology Products*, June 10, 2013

NSTISSP 200, *National Policy on Controlled Access Protection*, July 15, 1987

NSA/CSS Policy Manual 9-12, *NSA/CSS Storage Device Declassification Manual,* March 13, 2006

CJCSI 6211.02D, *Defense Information System Network (DISN) Responsibilities,* January 24, 2012

CJCSI 6510.01F, *Information Assurance (Cybersecurity) and Computer Network Defense (CND)*, February 9, 2011

CJCSM 6510.01B, *Cyber Incident Handling Program*, July 10, 2012

Joint Publication (JP) 1-02, *Department of Defense Dictionary of Military and Associated Terms*, December 15, 2014

X.509 Certificate Policy for United States Department of Defense, February 9, 2005

FIPS140-2, *Security Requirements for Cryptographic Modules,* May 25, 2001

DoDM 1000.13 v1, *DoD Identification (ID) Cards: ID Card Life-Cycle*, DoDI 1000.13, *Identification (ID) Cards for Members of the Uniformed Services, Their Dependents, and Other Eligible Individuals,* DISA Security Technical Implementation Guides (STIGs), **http://iase.disa.mil/stigs/**

DoD Antivirus Solutions, **http://www.disa.mil/antivirus/index.html**

DoD Policy Memorandum, *Mobile Code Technologies Risk Category List Update*, March 14, 2011, **https://powhatan.iiie.disa.mil/mcp/mcpdocs.html**

DoD CIO Memorandum, *DoD Commercial Mobile Device Implementation Plan*, February 15, 2013

DoDI 4161.02, *Accountability and Management of Government Contract Property,* April 27, 2012

DoDI 5000.02, *Operation of the Defense Acquisition System*, January 7, 2015

DoDM 5200.01, Volume 1, *DoD Information Security Program: Overview, Classification, and Declassification*, February 24, 2012

DoDM 5200.01, Volume 2, *DoD Information Security Program: Marking of Classified Information*, February 24, 2012

DoDM 5200.01, Volume 3, *DoD Information Security Program: Protection of Classified Information*, February 24, 2012

DoDM 5200.01, Volume 4, *DoD Information Security Program: Controlled Unclassified Information (CUI)*, February 24, 2012

DoDI 5200.02,*DoDPersonnel Security Program (PSP),* March 21, 2014

DoDI 5200.08, *Security of DoD Installations and resources and the DoD Physical Security Review Board (PSRB),* December 10, 2005

DoD 8570.01-M, *Information Assurance Workforce Improvement Program*, January 24, 2012

DoDI 3200.12, *DoD Scientific and Technical Information Program (STIP)*, August 22, 2013

DoDD 5230.11, *Disclosure of Classified Military Information to Foreign Governments and International Organizations,* June 16, 1992

DoDD 5230.20, *Visits and Assignments of Foreign Nationals,* June 22, 2005

DoDD 5230.25, *Withholding of Unclassified Technical Data from Public Disclosure*, August 18, 1995

DoDD 5400.7, *DoD Freedom of Information Act (FOIA) Program*, July 28, 2011

DoDD 8000.01, *Management of the Department of Defense Information Enterprise*, February 10, 2009

DoDD 8100.2, *Use of Commercial Wireless Devices, Services, and Technologies in the Department of Defense (DoD) Global Information Grid (GIG)*, April 14, 2004

DoDD 8500.01, *Cybersecurity*, March 14, 2014

DoDD 8521.01, *Department of Defense Biometrics,* February 21, 2008

DoDI 1035.01, *Telework Policy*, April 4, 2012

DoDI 1100.21, *Voluntary Services in the Department of Defense,* December 26, 2002

DoDI 5134.16, *Deputy Assistant Secretary of Defense for Systems Engineering* (DASD(SE))," August 19, 2011

DoDI 5205.08, *Access to Classified Cryptographic Information*, November 8, 2007

DoDI 5205.13, *Defense Industrial Base (DIB) Cyber Security/Information Assurance (CS/Cybersecurity) Activities*, January 29, 2010

DoDI 8420.01, *Commercial Wireless Local-Area Network (WLAN) Devices, Systems, and Technologies,* November 3, 2009

DoDI 8510.01, *DoD Risk Management Framework (RMF),* March 12, 2014

DoDI 8520.02, *Public Key Infrastructure (PKI) and Public Key (PK) Enabling,* May 24, 2011

DoDI 8520.03, *Identity Authentication for Information Systems,* May 13, 2011

DoDI O-8530.2, *Support to Computer Network Defense, (CND),* March 9, 2001

DoDI 8540.01, *Cross Domain (CD) Policy,* May 8, 2015

DoDI 8550.01, *DoD Internet Services and Internet-based Capabilities*, September 11, 2012

DoDI 8551.01, *Ports, Protocols, and Services Management (PPSM)*,May 28, 2014

DoDI 8580.1, *Information Assurance (Cybersecurity) in the Defense Acquisition System*, July 9, 2004

DoDI 8581.01, *Information Assurance (Cybersecurity) Policy for Space Systems Used by the Department of Defense,* June 8, 2010

DoDI 8582.01, *Security of Unclassified DoD Information on Non-DoD Information Systems,* June 6, 2012

USCYBERCOM Communications Tasking Orders (CTOs), https://www.cybercom.mil/default.aspx

AFPD 33-2, Information Assurance (Cybersecurity) Program, August 3, 2011

AFI 10-701, Operations Security (OPSEC), June 8, 2011

AFI 10-710, Information Operations Condition (INFOCON), August 10, 2006

AFI 10-712, Telecommunications Monitoring and Assessment Program (TMAP), June 8, 2011

AFI 16-107, Military Personnel Exchange Program, February 2, 2006

AFI 16-201, Air Force Foreign Disclosure and Technology Transfer Program, July 23, 2014

AFJI 31-102, *Physical Security*, May 31, 1991

AFI 31-401, Information Security Program Management, November 1, 2005

AFI 31-501, Personnel Security Program Management, January 27, 2005

AFI 31-601, Industrial Security Program Management, June 29, 2005

AFMAN 33-153, *Information Technology Asset Management (ITAM),* Mar 19, 2014

AFI 33-115, Information Technology Service Management

AFMAN 33-283, *Communications Security (COMSEC) Operations*, September 3, 2014

AFMAN 33-210, *Air Force Assessment and Authorization (A&A) Program (AFAAP), TBD),* December 23, 2008

AFI 33-332, Air Force Privacy and Civil Liberties Program, January 12, 2015

AFI 33-360, Publications and Forms Management, September 25, 2013

AFI 33-401, Air Force Architecting, May 17, 2011

AFI 36-2201, Air Force Training Program, September 15, 2010

AFI 36-3026_IP, Volume 1, Identification (ID) Cards for Members of the Uniformed Services, Their Eligible Family Members, and Other Eligible Personnel, June 17, 2009

AFI 63-101/20-101, Integrated Life Cycle Management, March 7, 2013

AFI 71-101 Volume 3, The Air Force Technical Surveillance Countermeasures Program, January 16, 2013

AFI 90-201, The Air Force Inspection System, August 2, 2013

AFKAG-2L, (FOUO) *Air Force COMSEC Accounting Manual*, May 15, 2007

AFMAN 33-145, *Collaboration Services and Voice Systems Management,* September 6, 2012

AFMAN 33-152, *User Responsibilities and Guidance for Information Systems*, June 1, 2012

AFMAN 33-285, *Information Assurance (Cybersecurity) Workforce Improvement Program,* June 17, 2011

AFMAN 33-363, *Management of Records*, March 1, 2008

AFMAN 33-407, *Air Force Clinger-Cohen Act (CCA) Compliance Guide*, 24 October 2012*Air Force Records Information Management System Records Disposition Schedule (RDS)*

AFSPC/A6 Combined Implementation Guidance for USCYBERCOM CTO 10-084 and 10-133 Memorandum, July 6, 2011

624 OC TASKORD 2012-76-014, *Classified Message Incident (CMI) Declaration Authority & Handling Procedures*

MPTO 00-33A-1109, *Vulnerability Management*

MPTO 00-33B-5004, *Access Control for Information Systems*

MPTO 00-33B-5006, *End point Security for Information Systems*

MPTO 00-33B-5008, *Remanence Security for Information Systems*

MPTO 00-33D-2001, *Active Directory Naming Conventions*

T.O. 00-33A-1202-WA-1, *Air Force Network Account Management,* May 12, 2011

T.O. 31S5-4-7255-8-1, *Configuration and Operations Guide for Air Force Certificate-Based Smart Card Logon / Next Generation Using Personal Identity Verification (PIV) Certificate*

TO 31S5-4-7256-8-1, *Configuration and Operations Guide for Air Force Certificate-Based Smart Card Logon / Next Generation Using Alternate Security Identification (ALTSECID)*

Prescribed Forms:

AF Form 4167, Two-Person Control (TPC) COMSEC Material Inventory

AF Form 4170, Emission Security Assessments/Emission Security Countermeasures Reviews

Adopted Forms:

SF 312, Nondisclosure Agreement

SF 700, Security Container Information Form

DD Form 2875, System Authorization Access Request (SAAR)

DD Form 2946, DoD Telework Agreement

AF Form 4394, Air Force User Agreement Statement-Notice and Consent Provision

AF Form 847, Recommendation for Change of Publication

Abbreviations and Acronyms

AF —Air Force (as used in forms)

AF CTTA —Certified TEMPEST Technical Authority (CTTA)

AFCTAG -- AF —Cybersecurity Technical Advisory Group

AFI —Air Force Instruction

AFIA —Air Force Inspection Agency

AFIN —Air Force Information Networks

AFIS —Air Force Inspection Service

AFKAG —Air Force Cryptographic Aid, General

AFMAN —Air Force Manual

AFNET —The Air Force's underlying Non-Secure Internet Protocol Router Network (NIPRNet)

AFNET-S —The Air Force's underlying Secure Internet Protocol Router Network (SIPRNet)

AFNIC —Air Force Network Integration Center

AFOSI —Air Force Office of Special Investigations

AFPC —Air Force Personnel Center

AFPD —Air Force Policy Directive

AFRIMS —Air Force Records Information Management System

AFRMC —Air Force Risk Management Council

AFSC —Air Force Specialty Code

AFSPC —Air Force Space Command

AFSSI —Air Force Systems Security Instruction

ALT —Alternate Logon Token

ALTSECID —Alternate Security Identification

AIS —Automated Information System

AO —Authorizing Official

ATO —Authorization to Operate

A&A —Assessment & Authorization (formerly C&A)

C2 —Command and Control

CA —Certificate Authority

CAC —Common Access Card

CAM —COMSEC Account Manager

CAP —Cryptographic Access Program

CCB —Configuration Control Board

CCEVS —Common Criteria Evaluation and Validation Scheme

CDC —Cleared Defense Contractors

CDS —Cross-Domain Solutions

CDSE —Cross Domain Service Element

CDSO —Cross Domain Solution Office

CE —Computing Environment

CHVP —Cryptographic High Value Products

CI —Counterintelligence

CIA —Confidentiality, Integrity, Availability

CIO —Chief Information Officer

CITS —Combat Information Transport System

CJCSI —Chairman of the Joint Chiefs of Staff Instruction

CJCSM —Chairman of the Joint Chiefs of Staff Manual

CM —Configuration Management

CMI —Classified Message Incident

CMVP —Cryptographic Module Validation Program

CND —Computer Network Defense

CNSSI —Committee on National Security Systems Instruction

CNSSP —Committee on National Security Systems Policy

COCOM —Combatant Command

COI —Community of Interest

COMPUSEC —Computer Security

COMSEC —Communications Security

CoN —Certificate of Networthiness

CTO —Communications Tasking Order

CTS —Computerized Telephone Switch

CTTA —Certified TEMPEST Technical Authority

CUI —Controlled Unclassified Information

Cybersecurity —Information Assurance

CybersecurityAP —Cybersecurity Assessment and Assistance Program

CYSS —Cyberspace Support Squadron

DAMO —Damage Assessment Management Office

DaR —Data at Rest

DC3 —Department of Defense Cyber Crime Center

DCS —Defense Collaboration Services

DFARS —Defense Federal Acquisition Regulation Supplement

DIB —Defense Industrial Base

DISA —Defense Information Systems Agency

DoD —Department of Defense

DoDD —Department of Defense Directive

DoDI —Department of Defense Instruction

DoDIN —Department of Defense Information Network

DRU —Direct Reporting Unit

DSAWG —Defense Information Assurance Security Accreditation Working Group

DSS —Defense Security Service

DVD —Digital Versatile Disc

EIEMA —Enterprise Information Environment Mission Area

EITDR —Enterprise Information Technology Data Repository

eMASS —Enterprise Mission Assurance Support Service

EMSEC —Emission Security

EPL —Evaluated Products List

FAR —Federal Acquisition Regulation

FIPS —Federal Information Processing Standards

FISMA —Federal Information Management Security Act

FOA —Field Operating Agency

FOIA —Freedom of Information Act

FOUO —For Official Use Only

GIG —Global Information Grid

GWP —GIG Waiver Panel

HAF —Headquarters Air Force

HBSS —Host Based Security System

HIPAA —Health Insurance Portability and Accountability Act

HQ —Headquarters

HQ AETC —Headquarters Air Education and Training Command

HQ AFSPC —Headquarters Air Force Space Command

IAM —Information Assurance Manager

IAO —Information Assurance Officer

IAW —In accordance with

ICD —Intelligence Community Directive

ID —Identification

IMT —Information Management Technology

INFOCON —Information Condition

IPT —Integrated Process Teams

IS —Information System

ISSM —Information System Security Manager

ISO —Information System Owner

ISSE —Information System Security Engineering/ Engineer

ISSM —Information System Security Manager

ISSO —Information System Security Officer

IT —Information Technology

JP —Joint Publication

KMI —Key Management Infrastructure

KS —Knowledge Service

LRA —Local Registration Authority

MAO —Mission Area Owner (Component [AF] level PAO)

MAJCOM —Major Command

MFD —Multifunction Device

MICT —Management Control Internal Tool

MOU —Memorandum of Understanding

MPTO —Methods and Procedures Technical Orders

NC3 —Nuclear Command Control and Communications

NIPRNet —Non-Secure Internet Protocol Router Network

NIST —National Institute of Standards and Technology

NSTISSI —National Security Telecommunications and Information Systems Security Instruction

NSTISSP —National Security Telecommunications and Information Systems Security Policy

NTSWG —National Telephone Security Working Group

NSA —National Security Agency

NSA/CSS —National Security Agency/Central Security Service

NSS —National Security System

OMB —Office of Management and Budget

OPR —Office of Primary Responsibility

OPSEC —Operations Security

OSI —Office of Special Investigations

PAO —Principle Authorizing Official

PED —Portable Electronic Device

PEO —Program Executive Officer

PII —Personally Identifiable Information

PIN —Personal Identification Number

PIT —Platform Information Technology

PIV —Personal Identity Verification

PIV-I —Personal Identity Verification-Interoperable

PK —Public-Key

PKCS —Public-Key Cryptography Standards

PKI —Public Key Infrastructure

PM —Program Manager

PMO —Program Management Office

POA&M —Plan of Actions and Milestones

PPS —Ports, Protocol, and Services

PPSM —Ports, Protocol, and Services Management

RDS —Records Disposition Schedule

RMF —Risk Management Framework

SAAR —System Authorization Access Request

SACs —Self-Assessments Communicators

SAF —Secretary of the Air Force

SAISO —Senior Agency Information Security Officer

SAP/SAR —Special-Access Program/Special Access Required

SCA —Security Control Assessor

SCAR -- SCA —Representatives

SCI —Sensitive Compartmented Information

SCIF —Sensitive Compartmentalized Information Facility

SDLC —Software Development Life Cycle

SECAF —Secretary of the Air Force

SF —Standard Form

SIPRNet —Secret Internet Protocol Router Network

SISO —Senior Information Security Officer

SME —Subject Matter Expert

SME PED —Secure Mobile Environment Portable Electronic Device

SPO —System Program Office

SP —Special Publications

STIG —Security Technical Implementation Guide

STIP —Scientific and Technical Information Program

SVRO —Secure Voice Responsible Officers

SwA —Software Assurance

TAG —Technical Advisory Group

TDY —Temporary Duty

TMAP —Telecommunications Monitoring and Assessment Program

TO —Technical Order

TSCM —Technical Surveillance Countermeasures

UC —Unified Capabilities

UC APL —Unified Capabilities Approved Products List

UCDSMO —Unified Cross Domain Services Management Office

US —United States

USB —Universal Serial Bus

U.S.C. —United States Code

USCYBERCOM —United States Cyber Command

USSTRATCOM —United States Strategic Command

USM —Unit Security Manager

VoLAC —Volunteer Logical Access Credential

VPN —Virtual Private Network

VTC —Video Teleconferencing

WCO —Wing Cybersecurity Office

WIP —Workforce Improvement Program

WLAN —Wireless Local Area Network

Terms

AF CTTA —(Air Force Certified TEMPEST Technical Authority) An experienced, technically qualified government employee who has met established certification requirements according to CNSS-approved criteria (see CNSSP-300 and CNSSI 7000 (C/REL)), and is appointed by SAF/CIO A6 SISO to fulfill CTTA responsibilities. (AFMAN 33-286).

AFCTAG —(Air Force Cyber Security Technical Advisory Group) provides technical cybersecurity subject matter experts (SMEs) from across the MAJCOMs and functional communities to facilitate the management, oversight, and execution of the AF Cybersecurity Program. (See Figure 3.1).

AFIN —(Air Force Information Network) The globally interconnected, end-to-end set of Air Force information capabilities, and associated processes for collecting, processing, storing, disseminating, and managing information on-demand to warfighters, policy-makers, and support personnel, including owned, leased and contracted communications and computing systems and services, software (including applications), data, security services, other associated services, and national security systems. (AFI 10-1701).

AFRMC —(Air Force Risk Management Council) Provides a forum for senior cybersecurity professionals to validate and vet issues concerning cybersecurity risk from a mission and business perspective. (See Figure 3.1).

ALT —(Alternate Logon Token) A portable, user-controlled, physical device used to generate, store, and protect cryptographic information, and to perform cryptographic functions. (AFMAN 33-282).

AO —(Authorizing Official) A senior (federal) official or executive with the authority to formally assume responsibility for operating an information system at an acceptable level of risk to organizational operations (including mission, functions, image, or reputation), organizational assets, individuals, other organizations, and the Nation. (CNSSI 4009).

ATO —(Authorization to Operate) The official management decision given by a senior organizational official to authorize operation of an information system and to explicitly accept the risk to organizational operations (including mission, functions, image, or reputation), organizational assets, individuals, other organizations, and the Nation based on the implementation of an agreed-upon set of security controls. (NIST 800-37, Rev. 1).

A&A —(Assessment & Authorization) (formerly C&A) The process by which organizations: (i) categorize information and information systems; (ii) select security controls; (iii) implement security controls; (iv) assess security control effectiveness; (v) authorize the information system; and (vi) [conduct] ongoing monitoring of security controls and the security state of the information system. (NIST 800-37, p. 4 *adapted*).

CND —(Computer Network Defense) Actions taken to defend against unauthorized activity within computer networks. CND includes monitoring, detection, analysis (such as trend and pattern analysis), and response and restoration activities. (CNSSI 4009).

CTO —(Cyber Tasking Order) An operational type order issued to perform specific actions at specific time frames in support of AF and Joint requirements. (AFI 10-1701).

Cybersecurity —(Information Assurance) Prevention of damage to, protection of, and restoration of computers, electronic communications systems, electronic communications services, wire communication, and electronic communication, including information contained therein, to ensure its availability, integrity, authentication, confidentiality, and nonrepudiation. (CNSSI 4009).

CYSS —(Cyberspace Support Squadron) Provides cyber networking expertise to AFSPC for Cyberspace Lead MAJCOM activities and functions.

DAMO —(Damage Assessment Management Office) Conducts damage assessments by collaboratively analyzing information compromised as a result of cyber intrusions to Defense Industrial Base information systems to determine overall impact to current and future Air Force weapons programs, scientific and research projects, and warfighting capabilities. (DoDI 5205.13, *adapted*).

DaR —(Data at Rest) Information that resides on electronic media while excluding data that is traversing a network or temporarily residing in computer memory to be read or updated. Data at rest can be archival or reference files that are changed rarely or never. Data at rest also includes data that is subject to regular but not constant change. (DoDI 8580.02-R).

DC3 —(Department of Defense Cyber Crime Center) Provides digital and multimedia (D/MM) forensics, cyber investigative training, research, development, test and evaluation (RDT&E), and cyber analytics for the following DoD mission areas: information assurance (IA) and critical infrastructure protection (CIP), law enforcement and counterintelligence (LE/CI), document and media exploitation (DOMEX), and counterterrorism (CT). (**https://www.dc3.mil/index/about-dc3**).

EIEMA —(Enterprise Information Environment Mission Area) IEMA is the DoD information (IT) portfolio that manages investments in the current and future integrated information sharing, computing and communications environment of the Air Force Information Network (AFIN). The IE comprises AFIN assets that operate as, provide information transport for, perform enterprise management of, and assure various levels and segments of the enterprise network, ranging from local area to wide area networks and from tactical to operational and strategic networks. The domains are Communications, Computing Infrastructure, Core Enterprise Services, and Information Assurance. (DoD CIO Memorandum, *Enterprise Information Environment Mission Area (EIEMA) Domain Owner Designations*, dated July 14, 2004).

EITDR —(Enterprise Information Technology Data Repository) EITDR is the Air Force IT Portfolio Management system of record. EITDR is accessible through the Air Force Portal. EITDR contains a current inventory of initiatives, systems, and system-related data and is used for internal management and oversight as well as to provide information to external sources to satisfy statutory and regulatory requirements. (AFI 33-141)

eMASS —(Enterprise Mission Assurance Support Service) eMASS is a government-owned, government-off-the-shelf (GOTS) web-based application, which supports cybersecurity program management. EMASS is fully compliant with security controls-based cybersecurity.

eMASS is designed to operate in either the Unclassified but Sensitive Internet Protocol Router Network (NIPRNet) enclave or the Secret Internet Protocol Router Network (SIPRNet) enclave. eMASS is public-key enabled (PKE) and all data in transit is fully encrypted. (**https://emass-airforce.csd.disa.mil/Content/Help/eMASS%205.1%20User%20Guide.pdf**).

ISO —(Information System Owner) Official responsible for the overall procurement, development, integration, modification, or operation and maintenance of an information system. (CNSSI 4009).

ISSE —(Information System Security Engineering/ Engineer) Individual assigned responsibility for conducting information system security engineering activities. (NIST 800-37).

ISSM —(Information System Security Manager) Individual responsible for the cybersecurity of a program, organization, system, or enclave. (CNSSI 4009)

ISSO —(Information System Security Officer) Individual assigned responsibility by the senior agency information security officer (SISO), authorizing official, management official, or information system owner for maintaining the appropriate operational security posture for an information system or program. (CNSSI 4009).

IT —(Information Technology) (A) The term "information technology," with respect to an executive agency means any equipment or interconnected system or subsystem of equipment, that is used in the automatic acquisition, storage, manipulation, management, movement, control, display, switching, interchange, transmission, or reception of data or information by the executive agency. For purposes of the preceding sentence, equipment is used by an executive agency if the equipment is used by the executive agency directly or is used by a contractor under a contract with the executive agency which (i) requires the use of such equipment, or (ii) requires the use, to a significant extent, of such equipment in the performance of a service or the furnishing of a product.

(B) The term "information technology" includes computers, ancillary equipment, software, firmware and similar procedures, services (including support services), and related resources. (40 U.S.C., Sec. 1401)

MAO —(Mission Area Owner) The person responsible for a defined area of responsibility with functions and processes that contribute to mission accomplishment. (DoDD 8115.01).

PED —(Portable Electronic Device) Electronic devices having the capability to store, record, and/or transmit text, images/video, or audio data. Examples of such devices include, but are not limited to: pagers, laptops, cellular telephones, radios, compact disc and cassette players/recorders, portable digital assistant, audio devices, watches with input capability, and reminder recorders. (ICS 700-1)

PIT —(Platform Information Technology) IT, both hardware and software, that is physically part of, dedicated to, or essential in real time to the mission performance of special purpose systems. (DoDI 8500.01).

RMF —(Risk Management Framework) A structured approach used to oversee and manage risk for an enterprise. (CNSSI 4009).

SCA —(Security Control Assessor) The individual, group, or organization responsible for conducting a security control assessment. (NIST 800-37).

Security Control Assessment —The testing and/or evaluation of the management, operational, and technical security controls in an information system to determine the extent to which the controls are implemented correctly, operating as intended, and producing the desired outcome with respect to meeting the security requirements for the system. (NIST 800-37).

SISO —(Senior Information Security Officer) Official responsible for carrying out the chief information officer (CIO) responsibilities under the Federal Information Security Management Act (FISMA) and serving as the CIO's primary liaison to the agency's authorizing officials, information system owners, and information systems security officers. (CNSSI 4009).

BY ORDER OF THE
SECRETARY OF THE AIR FORCE

AIR FORCE INSTRUCTION 33-150

30 NOVEMBER 2011
Incorporating Change 1, 18 December 2014

Communications and Information

*MANAGEMENT OF CYBERSPACE
SUPPORT ACTIVITIES*

COMPLIANCE WITH THIS PUBLICATION IS MANDATORY

ACCESSIBILITY: Publications and forms are available on the e-Publishing website at
www.e-Publishing.af.mil for downloading or ordering.

RELEASABILITY: There are no releasability restrictions on this publication.

OPR: SAF/A6ONI

Certified by: SAF/A6ON
(Col Daniel Elmore)
Pages: 29

Supersedes: AFI33-150, 26 November 2008 and
AFI33-104, 10 May 2001

This Air Force Instruction (AFI) implements Air Force Policy Directive AFPD 33-1, *Cyberspace Support*. It establishes the management of cyberspace resources to include systems, equipment, personnel, time, and money and provides the directive guidance for Air Force cyberspace support activities. This publication applies to all military and civilian Air Force personnel, members of the Air Force Reserve Command (AFRC), Air National Guard (ANG), third-party governmental employee and contractor support personnel in accordance with appropriate provisions contained in memoranda support agreements and Air Force contracts. In this document, the term "cyberspace support activity" is defined as any action taken to restore communications systems/equipment to operational status, to perform preventive maintenance inspections (PMI) on communications systems/equipment and/or components, or to install or remove communications systems/equipment. The term cyberspace infrastructure refers to equipment and network infrastructure to provide the internet, network operations and command and control, and embedded processors and controllers. The term "Communications systems/equipment" is defined as: transmission, switching, processing, systems-control, and network management systems, as well as equipment, software, and facilities, fixed and deployable, that supports a mission area. The intent of this instruction is to ensure only qualified personnel perform cyberspace support activities and prevent damage to communications hardware, software, stored information, and current mission operations. One or more paragraphs of this AFMAN may not apply to non-AF-managed joint service systems. These paragraphs are marked as follows: *(NOT APPLICABLE TO NON-AF-MANAGED JOINT SERVICE SYSTEMS)*. The authorities to waive wing/unit level requirements in this publication are identified with a

Tier ("T-0, T-1, T-2, T-3") number following the compliance statement. See AFI 33-360, *Publications and Forms Management*, Table 1.1 for a description of the authorities associated with the Tier numbers. Submit requests for waivers through the chain of command to the appropriate Tier waiver approval authority, or alternately, to the Publication OPR for non-tiered compliance items. Send recommended changes or comments using AF Form 847, *Recommendation for Change of Publication*, to Cyberspace Strategy and Policy Division (SAF/A6SS), 1030 Air Force Pentagon, Washington DC 20330-1030. When collecting and maintaining information protect it by the Privacy Act of 1974 authorized by 10 U.S.C. 8013. Ensure that all records created as a result of processes prescribed in this publication are maintained in accordance with Air Force Manual (AFMAN) 33-363, *Management of Records* and disposed of in accordance with Air Force Records Disposition Schedule (RDS) located in the Air Force Records Information Management System (AFRIMS). See Attachment 1 for a glossary of references and supporting information.

SUMMARY OF CHANGES

This interim change (1) incorporates responsibilities of Installation Communication Squadron (CS) Commanders and Tenant Unit Commanders previously documented in AFI 33-101, *Commanders Guidance and Responsibilities* (rescinded); (2) adds AF Data Center Consolidation responsibilities and guidance previously identified via AF Guidance Memorandum; (3) updates office symbol and responsibilities for 38th Cyberspace Engineering Installation Group (38 CEIG); (4) adds requires for AFTO Form 747, *Cyberspace Infrastructure Systems Acceptance*, and AFTO Form 229, *Engineering Installation Assistance*; (5) adds Tier waiver approval authorities according to AFI 33-360; (6) removes ATCALS references based on transfer to AF/A3. A margin bar (|) indicates newly revised material.

1. Purpose. This instruction implements new communications systems/equipment activity guidelines and changes or eliminates the requirement to complete redundant procedures and practices. Guidance in this publication is intended to assist Air Force personnel in identifying activities required to support Air Force communications. This instruction is an initiative to reduce the number of SAF/CIO A6 departmental- level publications by changing their publications from "stove-piped" system/program-based to audience/role-based focus. Specific procedural information is located in the more detailed Methods and Procedures Technical Orders (MPTO) or specialized publications. Common core communication services for standard user information (e.g., e-mail, phone, messaging, etc.) are located in AFMAN 33-152, *Users Responsibilities and Guidance for Information Systems*. Guidance for acquisition and sustainment planning is located in AFI 63-101, *Integrated Life Cycle Management*.

1.1. **Objectives**. The primary objectives of cyberspace support activities are to ensure continuous security, operational availability, and reliability of systems and equipment supporting the Air Force mission. This instruction outlines unit roles and responsibilities to ensure communications systems/equipment are serviceable and properly configured to meet mission requirements.

1.2. **Intent.** This instruction mandates the use of MPTO 00-33A-1001, *General Cyberspace Support Activities Management Procedures and Practice Requirements*, which establishes implementation guidance and procedures; MPTO 00-33D-3003, *Managing the Cyberspace Infrastructure with the Cyberspace Infrastructure Planning System*, which explains how to use the Cyberspace Infrastructure Planning System (CIPS) to document, fund, distribute, implement, and manage the cyberspace infrastructure; and MPTO 33D-2002, *Engineering, Implementation, and Cyberspace Readiness Activities Management*, which defines the processes and procedures for the management of Engineering Installation (EI) and Cyberspace Readiness activities to include providing Major Commands (MAJCOMs) and bases with the necessary information to process EI requirements for funding via the Air Force (AF) EI Work Plan in CIPS. These elements support the objectives in **paragraph 1.1**. **Note:** This AFI and supporting MPTOs cannot alter or supersede the existing authorities and policies of the Director of National Intelligence (DNI) regarding the protection of Sensitive Compartmented Information (SCI) systems or intelligence, surveillance, reconnaissance mission and mission support systems. This AFI and supporting MPTOs cannot alter or supersede higher authoritative guidance governing Special Access Program (SAP) systems, counterintelligence or law enforcement collection operations, or investigations involving communication systems. When DNI or SAP authorities fail to address areas covered by this AFI, this AFI and associated MPTOs need be followed. If there is conflict between this AFI and associated MPTOs with guidance issued by DNI or SAP authorities, DNI or SAP guidance will precedence. TOs are available for ordering through the Enhanced Technical Information System (ETIMS) application on the AF Portal, per TO 00-5-1, *Air Force Technical Order System*. Contact unit Technical Order Distribution Office (TODO) for assistance.

2. Roles and Responsibilities. Note: For this instruction, the term major command (MAJCOM) also applies to Numbered Air Forces (NAF), Field Operating Agencies (FOA) and Direct Reporting Units (DRU).

2.1. **Chief Information Dominance and Chief Information Officer(SAF/CIO A6).** Develops and publishes cyberspace support activities, strategy, policy, tactical doctrine, and programs to integrate warfighting and combat support capabilities, and oversees implementation of enterprise information, information resources, and data management capabilities for Joint, Coalition and Air Force warfighters. Coordinates with military services, MAJCOMs and any additional government agencies as applicable. In addition, SAF/CIO A6 will:

2.1.1. Manage cyberspace operations career fields.

2.1.2. Act as the approval authority for waiver requests to deviate from the requirements of this publication.

2.1.3. DELETED.

2.1.4. Appoint executive agent for IT emerging technologies.

2.1.5. Establish overall guidance, act as approval authority for plans, and resolve proposed consolidation actions for Centralized Repair Activities (CRA).

2.1.6. Act as the approval authority for:

2.1.6.1. Proposed temporary T-1 AFNET system/equipment modifications according to AFI 63-131, *Modification Management*.

2.1.7. Will oversee management and disposition of all AF data centers as described in **paragraph 3**, to include the data center components of weapons systems.

2.1.7.1. Ensure all requirements support the Federal Data Center Consolidation Initiative (FDCCI) IAW **paragraph 3**.

2.1.7.2. Coordinate with AFSPC and other Lead MAJCOMs to determine if existing capabilities across the AF or DoD will satisfy the requirement. Requests satisfied by existing capabilities will be disapproved and returned to the requestor along with appropriate rationale and recommended alternatives IAW **paragraph 3**.

2.2. **Air Force Space Command (AFSPC).** As Lead Command for all Air Force Cyberspace Operations via the 24AF(AFCYBER), AFSPC will be the Air Force focal point for establishment, operation, maintenance, defense, exploitation, and attack Cyberspace Operations. AFSPC coordinates the prioritization of all Cyberspace Infrastructure requirements. In addition, AFSPC will:

2.2.1. Control the membership of the Engineering and Installation Governance Structure (EIGS).

2.2.2. Coordinate the establishment of and the schedule for the EIGS composed of representatives from all MAJCOMs for the review, prioritization, and funding of EI projects Air Force-wide.

2.2.3. Ensure program information is documented in the CIPS.

2.2.4. Manage and distribute the consolidated funding for EI projects.

2.2.5. Manage and distribute the consolidated Military Personnel Appropriation (MPA) man-days for ANG implementation of projects.

2.2.6. In coordination with 38th Cyberspace Engineering Installation Group (38 CEIG), monitor the execution of cyberspace projects approved for implementation.

2.2.7. In coordination with the A6 community, develop, manage, and defend EI Program Objective Memorandum (POM) inputs with the information that resides in CIPS.

2.2.8. Support FDCCI goals and objectives when managing and distributing the consolidated funding for Engineering Installation (EI) projects.

2.3. **Air Force Network Integration Center.** As a Direct Reporting Unit to AFSPC, AFNIC is designated as the United States Air Force (USAF) lead agency to develop policy and guidance for cyberspace support activities and related areas to shape, provision, integrate and sustain the AF Cyber Network in all four domains: terrestrial, air, space and cyberspace. In addition, AFNIC will:

2.3.1. AFNIC Enterprise Systems Policy, Procedures and Support Division (ESP) will:

2.3.1.1. Manage assigned cyberspace support activities policy, procedures, and MPTO 00-33A-1001.

2.3.1.2. Manage all waiver requests relating to cyberspace support activities.

2.3.1.3. Manage the Air Force Communications Quality Control Checklist (AFCQCC) program.

2.3.1.4. Represent the communications personnel/community as members of workgroups, integrated process/product teams as required.

2.3.1.5. Serve as focal point for Air Force guidance and directives regarding communication systems/equipment modifications except when MAJCOM is designated as the Air Force Lead or lead command per paragraph 2.4.5.

2.3.1.6. Under direction from SAF/A6SF, develop compliance inspection criteria for the Air Force Inspector General (TIGs).

2.3.1.7. Act as focal point for Standard Reporting Designator assignment for non-Air Force Material Command (AFMC) centrally managed commercial items and/or Government-Off-The-Shelf (GOTS) equipment.

2.3.1.8. Manage Depot Purchased Equipment Maintenance, Low Density Level (LDL) assets, non-airborne Readiness Spares Packages (RSP), and provide material management assistance to units.

2.3.1.9. Provide enterprise level equipment analysis capability metrics, such as reliability, availability, and maintainability, utilizing approved automated information system (AIS).

2.3.1.10. Perform unit-funded staff assistance visit (SAVs) upon request and availability of manpower.

2.3.1.11. Manage Information Technology (IT) hardware asset accountability according to AFMAN 33-153, *Information Technology (IT) Asset Management (ITAM)*.

2.3.2. AFNIC Enterprise Systems Cyber Force Strategies (ESF) will:

2.3.2.1. Manage training resources in support of formal courses, upgrade training, certification training and newly integrated technology training.

2.3.2.2. Support cyberspace operations career fields and systems providing/managing computer based training, instructor led training, and virtual instructor led training.

2.3.3. AFNIC Enterprise Systems Maintenance Management (ESM) will:

2.3.3.1. Perform system management duties and responsibilities as specified in current Memoranda of Understanding (MOU), Memoranda of Agreement (MOA), and Service Level Agreements (SLA).

2.3.3.2. Review MAJCOM recommended changes to Air Force-managed programs, systems/equipment.

2.3.3.3. Assess, evaluate, and ensure compliance with governing directives for communications systems/equipment, as directed or requested.

2.3.3.4. AFNIC Integration Engineering (EN) will:

2.3.3.5. Direct engineering standards and solutions to configuration manage, control, integrate, and optimize Air Force network (AFNet) Cyberspace operations and the core services it provides.

2.3.3.6. Provide engineering analysis and assessment to characterize and resolve AFNet performance, integration, and interoperability issues to meet customer quality of service delivery expectations.

2.4. **Major Commands (MAJCOMs).** MAJCOMs implement Air Force guidance concerning their communications systems/equipment. MAJCOMs will:

2.4.1. Manage and provide support for command-unique programs and systems/equipment.

2.4.2. Coordinate MAJCOM policy, procedures, and Technical Order (T.O.) supplements for implementation consideration affecting cyberspace support activities, subject to the following conditions:

2.4.2.1. Supplements must not be less restrictive than higher level publications or the basic publications being supplemented, and must not contradict or conflict with Air Force-wide policy, procedure, or publications according to AFI 33-360, *Publications and Forms Management*.

2.4.2.2. Supplements must contain only MAJCOM unique material.

2.4.2.3. Recommended MAJCOM supplements to Air Force publications, forms, and checklists. Also, proposed changes to Air Force-wide communications systems/programs/equipment must be coordinated with the appropriate OPR or lead command.

2.4.3. DELETED.

2.4.4. Ensure logistics support and life-cycle management plans are developed for MAJCOM-acquired/ procured commercial-off-the-shelf (COTS) communications systems and equipment.

2.4.5. When designated as Air Force Lead (early development) or as lead command, serve as focal point to develop/implement Air Force guidance and directives concerning communications systems/ equipment.

2.4.6. Review and forward all waiver requests relating to communications systems/equipment activities to AFNIC/ES via AFSC 3DXXX Functional Managers.

2.4.7. Act as approval authority for MAJCOM-developed Local Communications Quality Control Checklist (LCQCCs) for command-unique programs, systems and equipment, IAW T.O. 00-33A-1001.

2.4.8. Provide quality assurance (QA) guidance, if required.

2.4.9. Manage and act as approval authority for support/maintenance assistance requests. Assistance requests may be accomplished if unit-funded and manpower is available.

2.4.10. Establish focal point for CRA management, if applicable.

2.4.11. Prioritize their own work plan(s) and provide representatives to the EIGS for the review, prioritization, and funding of projects Air Force-wide. Reference **paragraph 2.5** for EIGS structure and TO 33D-2002 for AF EI work plan process.

2.4.12. Designate appropriate system functional managers.

2.4.13. MAJCOMs owning, managing, or operating data centers as defined by OMB (servers in any form, except for those expressly exempted by this AFI) will ensure these facilities are documented in Data Center Inventory Management System (DCIMS) and all obligations to acquire IT are approved IAW the process in **paragraph 3**.

2.4.14. Coordinate any Defense Information Systems Network (DISN) Long-Haul Communications changes required to support data center and data server requests according to AFMAN 33-116, *Long-Haul Communications Management*.

2.5. **Engineering and Installation Governance Structure (EIGS).** EIGS organizations include the EIGS Council (composed of MAJCOM two-letter representatives), the EIGS Board (MAJCOM three-letter level), and the EIGS Group (MAJCOM four-letter level) which prioritize and approve EI requirements Air Force-wide. In addition, the EIGS will:

2.5.1. Provide senior leader guidance to Cyberspace program planners to help determine project priorities.

2.5.2. Develop minimum submission criteria, provide guidance, and set the schedule for cyberspace infrastructure work plans.

2.5.3. Establish the funding "cut line" for the EI PEC (Program Element Code) 27436F based on the amount disbursed.

2.5.4. Review the priorities, adjust them if needed, and approve a single consolidated Air Force-wide centralized EI work plan, considering both contractual implementation and organic implementation.

2.5.5. In coordination with 38th Cyberspace Engineering Installation Group (38 CEIG), monitor execution of approved EI requirements.

2.6. **38th Cyberspace Engineering Installation Group (38 CEIG).** The 38 CEIG and its squadrons plans, engineers, and delivers a survivable and resilient infrastructure to establish the cyberspace domain and assist the Air Force mission to conduct offensive and defensive air, space, and cyberspace operations. They provide engineering, planning, implementation, management, and consultation support to enable establishment of forward operating bases, combatant command, Air Force, and Joint service net-centric environment. Reference MPTO 00-33D-2002 for all 38 CEIG services and processes. In addition, the 38 CEIG will:

2.6.1. Provide Air Force-wide cyberspace infrastructure and health assessments to identify shortfalls and vulnerabilities.

2.6.2. Provide specialized engineering, operational engineering, and emergency maintenance/restoral.

2.6.3. Develop and maintain the Technology Infrastructure component of the AFNet Enterprise Architecture, describing and identifying the physical layer including, the functional characteristics, capabilities, and interconnections of the hardware, software, and communications.

2.6.4. Provide Combatant Commanders a Designated Operational Capability (DOC)-tasked 72-hour rapid-response EI force that is deployable worldwide.

2.6.5. Provide a specialized contracting activity that executes responsive acquisition strategies and compliant sourcing solutions in support of the AF Cyberspace Mission, and the Air Force Work Plan.

2.6.6. Provision, budget, and manage inter-base Long Haul Communications (reference AFMAN 33-116), DISN Subscription Services (DSS), Mobile Satellite Services (MSS) and Teleport Management, GSA FTS2001/Networx Requirements Manager, common user network connectivity oversight, last half-mile connectivity task orders, and AF's MAJCOM Circuit Management Office (CMO) (reference AFI 33-134, *Mobile Satellite Services Management*).

2.6.7. Provide enterprise system management support to base communications squadrons/flights, MAJCOMs, Lead Commands, and Air Staff, to include field technical expertise on systems and policy interpretation.

2.6.8. Provide Cyberspace Information Technology acquisition support, project and program implementation services, and requirements review, preparation, and processing to the AF, Numbered Air Force (NAF)/Air Force Forces (AFFOR), DoD, and other government agencies IAW AFPD 16-5, *Planning, Programming, Budgeting, and Execution Process*.

2.6.8.1. DELETED.

2.6.8.2. DELETED.

2.6.9. As the CIPS Program Management Office (PMO), chairs the CIPS Oversight Group.

2.6.9.1. DELETED.

2.6.9.2. DELETED.

2.6.9.3. DELETED.

2.6.10. DELETED.

2.6.11. DELETED.

2.6.12. DELETED.

2.6.13. DELETED.

2.6.14. DELETED.

2.7. **Program Managers.**

2.7.1. Program managers will document their program information in CIPS according to MPTO 00-33D-3003 and AFI 63-101. **(T-1).** However, information regarding data center infrastructure must be documented in DCIMS according to **paragraph 3. (T-0)**

2.7.2. Address data center consolidation, according to **paragraph 3**, in acquisition planning and plan for end state disposition prior to the next major increment or modification. **(T-0)**

2.7.3. All Program Offices owning, managing, or operating data centers as defined by OMB (servers in any form, except for those expressly exempted by this AFI) will ensure these facilities are documented in DCIMS and all obligations to acquire IT are approved IAW the process in **paragraph 3. (T-0)**

2.8. **Engineering and Installation (EI) Total Force Group (TFG).** The TFG consists of: one (1) Active-Duty Air Force unit (85 EIS), 15 Air National Guard (ANG) Squadrons, National Guard Bureau (NGB)/A6 EI Functional Area Manager (FAM), 251 CEIG, 253, CEIG, and 38 CEIG. The TFG provides the process to implement funded cyberspace infrastructure projects with organic resources. TFG enterprise oversight is the responsibility of NGB/A6 EI FAM and 38 CEIG. In addition, the TFG will:

2.8.1. Review EIGS prioritized projects and make recommendations for organic implementation.

2.8.2. Dispense EIGS approved projects for organic implementation.

2.9. **Communications Unit Commanders or Equivalent.**

2.9.1. Implement all applicable programs listed in MPTO 00-33A-1001. MPTO 00-33A-1001 topics include Quality Assurance Program, Control of Production, Communications Inspection, Corrosion Prevention and Control Program (CPCP), Historical Record Management, Life Cycle Management, Material Management, Publications Programs, Antenna Identification, Tool Management, Performance Metrics and Algorithms for Communications, Centralized Repair Activities (CRA), System Managers, Specialized Communications Teams (SCT), Common Communications Procedures, and Climbing Training Requirements, Equipment Control. **(T-2)**

2.9.2. Establish a QA work center directly under the Communications Unit Commander or Operations Group as appropriate. **(T-3)**

2.9.3. Assign an individual as the Wing/Base 3A1XX Administration Functional Manager for accession, training, classification, utilization, and career development of enlisted (3A1XX) personnel. NOTE: These personnel operate in every functional area and often do not work in the Wing/Base communications unit. Nevertheless, they are specialized extensions of the total capability for cyber support to the Air Force mission. **(T-1)**

2.9.4. Process and sign the AFTO Form 747, *Cyberspace Infrastructure Systems Acceptance*, for all cyberspace infrastructure installation actions. **(T-2)**

2.9.5. Serve as the focal point for the installation's cyberspace systems, equipment, and programs. **(T-2)**

2.9.5.1. Ensure applications, systems, and core enterprise services are hosted only in SAF/CIO A6-approved facilities as defined by **paragraph 3.2.3. (T-0)**

2.9.5.2. Ensure all systems/equipment supported by cyberspace support activities is tracked in the approved AIS to include antennas. **(T-2)**

2.9.5.3. Ensure only Air Force-approved AIS such as Integrated Maintenance Data System (IMDS), Remedy, Telephone Management System (TMS), CIPS, and Training Business Area (TBA) are used for all customer service requests/work orders and training documentation unless granted a higher headquarters waiver. **Note**: Follow approved security classification guide or authoritative SAP and DNI guidance when applicable. **(T-2)**

2.9.6. Meet the mission needs of assigned tenant units and geographically separated units (GSUs) not receiving support from another host wing, command, or Service. **(T-2)**

2.9.6.1. Manage the infrastructure for host systems and tenant systems as defined in support agreements. **(T-2)**

2.9.6.2. Review and assist with the development of tenant plans involving communications and information resources or activities. **(T-3)**

2.9.7. Develop cyberspace infrastructure annexes and appendices, for installation specific contingency plans and support plans. **(T-3)**

2.9.8. Validate the base blueprint in CIPS prior to Installation commander's endorsement (reference AFTO Form 330, *Base Blueprint Endorsement Checklist*). **(T-3)**

2.9.9. Be the "Approval Authority" for CIPS accounts IAW MPTO 00-33D-3003. **(T-3)**

2.9.10. Coordinate CSI visits with installation level Functional Area Managers (FAMs) and installation Civil Engineering Squadron planners. **(T-3)**

2.9.11. Manage and document base cyberspace infrastructure projects in CIPS for current and out years. Reference MPTO 00-33D-3003. **(T-2)**

2.9.11.1. Manage all Communications and Information Systems Installation Records (CSIR) for Cyber Operations and Transport Systems per MPTO 00-33A-1001 until CIPS is enhanced to provide that capability. **(T-2)**

2.9.11.2. Manage the Cable and Antenna Systems Communications Mission Data Set (CMDS) layer in the CIPS Visualization Component (CVC) per MPTO 00-33D-3004. **(T-2)**

2.9.11.3. Prioritize and approve projects on Work Plan submissions in CIPS as applicable.

2.9.11.4. Follow the process in MPTO 00-33D-2002 for including Cyberspace Infrastructure requirements in the AF EI Work Plan process. **(T-2)**

2.9.12. Initiate and process the AFTO Form 229, *Engineering Installation Assistance,* to request services not identified or funded on the AF EI Work Plan as defined in MPTO 00-33D-2002. **(T-2)**

2.9.13. DELETED.

2.10. **Flight Commander/Flight Chief or equivalents.** At a minimum, the Flight Commander and Flight Chief of cyberspace personnel will:

2.10.1. DELETED.

2.10.2. Direct PMIs to be accomplished IAW appropriate or established T.O.s or in the absence of T.O.s, commercial manuals or publications.

2.10.3. Publish local workcards (LWC) and/or checklists if required.

2.10.4. Waive the accomplishment or approve deviations of scheduled inspections (e.g., PMIs) under conditions listed in MPTO 00-33A-1001.

2.10.5. Increase frequency or scope of scheduled inspections (e.g., PMIs) or individual inspection requirements when, and if, required.

2.10.6. Coordinate with applicable agencies/units for cyberspace support activities impacting operations.

2.10.7. Authorize use of local CQCCs.

2.10.8. Manage cyberspace deployment processes for equipment, personnel and technical documents.

2.10.9. Serve as approval authority for cannibalization or controlled substitution activities.

2.11. **Work center Supervisors.** At a minimum, work center supervisors of cyberspace personnel will:

2.11.1. Ensure compliance with directives, technical publications, and supplements.

2.11.2. Ensure customer service requests and work orders reflect current system/equipment status.

2.11.3. Understand supervisors' roles and responsibilities in the QA program.

2.11.4. Secure and control government property to include tracking warranty information.

2.11.5. Coordinate scheduled support actions (e.g., Time Change Item (TCI), and Time Compliance Technical Order (TCTO), Time Compliance Network Order (TCNO), Maintenance Tasking Order (MTO), Network Tasking Order (NTO), etc.) with Communications Focal Point (CFP).

2.11.6. Appoint project coordinator [e.g., EI, self-help, Specialized Communications Team (SCT), CIPS], and ensure required duties are accomplished.

2.11.7. Manage test, measurement, and diagnostic equipment and other test equipment.

2.11.8. Establish a comprehensive safety program to include such programs as Radio Frequency Radiation, Hazard Material, Hazard Communication, confined space, facility grounding, lock out/tag out, and climbing training.

2.11.9. Manage work center corrosion prevention and control program (CPCP) and electrostatic discharge program according to MPTO 00-33A-1001.

2.11.10. Ensure work center logistics support management responsibilities are accomplished.

2.11.11. Maintain historical files and master inventories on communications systems/equipment in applicable AIS.

2.11.12. DELETED.

2.12. **Communications Focal Point (CFP).** In the base communications squadron/flight, the CFP is the combination of the Maintenance Operations Center (MOC), telephone helpdesk and the traditional network helpdesk functions. The CFP function has tactical control (TACON) of the client service team (CST) Work center. The CST unit commanders retain administrative control of CSTs. The CST Work center retains TACON of all CSTs assigned to the base. A separate MOC may exist at bases where cyber systems are assigned to an Operations Group in addition to equipment/systems assigned to Communications Group/Squadron. The standalone MOC will comply with applicable CFP responsibilities contained in TO 00-33A-1001. **Note:** CFP and Enterprise IT Service Desk (ESD) integration is contained in MPTO 00-33A-1001. The CFP will:

2.12.1. Manage customer service requests, work orders, and equipment status reporting.

2.12.1.1. Manage service requests, trouble tickets, and/or service incidents according to Control of Production procedures in MPTO 00-33A-1001.

2.12.1.2. Manage work orders according to procedures in TO 00-33D-3003. **Note:** Work Order Management System (WOMS) is an integrated tool that permits users to create, track, and process work orders within CIPS at both the base and MAJCOM levels, while keeping work orders and infrastructure requirements as separate business objects.

2.12.2. Provide a 24-hour contact number to customers/users and base Command Post.

2.12.3. Manage/review approved AIS management products for accuracy and analyzes data for negative trends.

2.12.4. Manage reports (e.g., situational reports (SITREP), communications statistics, etc.) and disseminate to appropriate personnel for action. The CFP will disseminate monthly ticket and activities information to the unit commander.

2.12.5. Document and control removal/replacement/cannibalization actions.

2.12.6. Act as focal point for depot maintenance requests.

2.12.7. Ensure master PMI schedule is entered into the AIS and includes antennas.

2.12.8. Review, direct, and monitor accomplishment of scheduled and unscheduled support actions (e.g., TCI, TCTO, TCNO, MTO, NTO, outages, etc).

2.12.9. Serve as focal point (i.e., sub-system manager) for the Air Force-approved AISs (e.g., IMDS, Remedy, etc.).

2.12.10. Develop procedures to sustain operations in the event of power failure, communications outage, etc.

2.12.11. Review all SLAs, MOAs, or MOUs for applicability and impact to current cyberspace support activities according to AFI 25-201, *Intra-Service, Intra-Agency, and Inter-Agency Support Agreements Procedures*.

2.12.12. Provide customers with reporting procedures for communications systems outages/problems.

2.12.13. Perform the Logistics Service Center (LSC) liaison duties of Mission Capable and Turn-Around (TRN) Monitors.

2.12.14. Act as the main interface with the AFNet ESD.

2.12.15. Forward all CIPS requirements to the appropriate authority for implementation.

2.13. **Quality Assurance (QA).** The QA program is responsible directly to the commander or deputy. The QA program applies to all cyberspace AFSCs who sustain systems. At a minimum, QA personnel will:

2.13.1. Provide assistance, advice, and authoritative references to work center supervisors and unit leadership.

2.13.2. Establish and maintain a technical publications program (e.g., technical orders, Air Force Network Standard Operating Procedures, etc.).

2.13.3. Manage Quality Assessments and Trend Analysis activities using Air Force approved systems.

2.13.4. Process material and T.O. deficiencies.

2.13.5. Review work center facility, systems installation, and equipment records management.

2.13.6. Perform technical reviews of modifications proposals and process valid proposals according to applicable directives.

2.13.7. Perform CPCP and electrostatic discharge (ESD) focal point duties according to MPTO 00-33A-1001.

2.13.8. Review locally devised checklists, operating instructions, publications, and directives annually.

2.13.9. Submit changes to various publications, T.O.s and other guidance.

2.13.10. Review statements of work where cyberspace support activities are outsourced.

2.13.11. Complete Air Force Job Qualification Standard (AFJQS) 3DXXX-201G, *Quality Assurance*, within 180 days of assuming responsibilities unless previously completed and documented. Use this AFJQS as a guide for training Quality Assurance Representative (QAR) personnel.

2.13.12. Validate and manage LWCs.

2.13.13. Use applicable AFCQCCs during evaluations according to MPTO 00-33A-1001.

2.13.14. Perform in-process, acceptance, deactivation, or transfer inspections on equipment/systems being overhauled, repaired, installed, removed, or newly acquired.

2.14. **Tenant Unit Commanders (or equivalent)** will:

2.14.1. Appoint a tenant communications responsible officer to serve as their single focal point and accountable officer for the cyberspace support systems of their respective activities. **(T-2)**

2.14.2. Define specific tenant and installation communications squadron commander (or equivalent) responsibilities in the support agreement or similar document. Upon appointment, unit commanders (or equivalent) notify the installation communications squadron commander (or equivalent). **(T-2)**

2.14.3. Coordinate with the installation communications squadron commander (or equivalent) to ensure their systems will integrate and interoperate, when necessary, with the DODIN, AFIN, AFNET or host base systems. **(T-2)**

2.14.4. Identify to the host installation, MAJCOM, and lead MAJCOM for Cyberspace Operations, the special engineering, installation, operation and/or maintenance requirements for NSS, SAP or SCI or other federal agency systems that are used by the tenant. **(T-2)**

2.15. **All Organizations.** All organizations owning, managing, or operating servers in any form (data centers as defined by OMB), except for those expressly exempted by **paragraph 3.2.1** or **paragraph 3.3.1** will work with the SAF/CIO A6 DCC Team (see **paragraph 3.4**) to ensure these facilities are documented in DCIMS and all obligations are approved IAW the process in **paragraph 3**. **(T-0)**

3. **Data Servers And Data Centers Approval Process.**

3.1. **AF Data Center Infrastructure Management.** Under the FDCCI, OMB defines a data center as a closet, room, floor or building for the storage, management, and dissemination of data and information. This definition has been further defined by the DOD CIO to include single and multiple server instantiations regardless of adherence to Uptime Institute or TIA-942 standards. While it is generally recognized that weapon systems may not be data centers, most weapon systems have an IT component that may constitute a data center or reside in a data center. Thus, a weapon system designation , in and of itself, does not justify an exemption from FDCCI, related data center legislation, DOD guidance, or the guidance contained in this AFI. The SAF/CIO A6 will oversee management and disposition of all AF data centers under the purview of aforementioned guidance, to include the data center components of weapons systems.

3.2. **AF Data Center Consolidation.** The DOD CIO, working under the purview of FDCCI guidance, requires all data centers (exceptions are noted below) to be documented in DCIMS. Records will be created and maintained by data center owners IAW guidance and training provided by the AF Data Center Consolidation team within SAF/CIO A6. Data center end states (discussed below) submitted by data center owners will be adjudicated and approved by SAF/CIO A6.

3.2.1. DCIMS Exemptions. The following items are exempt from FDCCI and do not require entry into DCIMS:

3.2.1.1. IT components constituting a data center that are onboard airborne platforms.

3.2.1.2. IT components constituting a tactical data center such as those contained in shelters.

3.2.1.3. IT components constituting a data center where the metadata (location, configuration, owner, etc.) is classified. Those systems are inventoried separately by the Director of National Intelligence.

3.2.2. Data Center End States. The following data center end states are defined by the DOD CIO and approved for use in DCIMS:

3.2.2.1. Core Data Center (CDC) – These locations are selected by the DOD CIO and operated by DISA.

3.2.2.2. Installation Processing Node (IPN) – Data centers required to host applications required for base operations where access does not transit the base boundary. IPNs will not allow connections from one base to another and there shall be no more than one (1) IPN per base or installation.

3.2.2.3. Special Purpose Processing Node (SPPN) – Servers connected to special purpose IT or non-IT equipment that cannot be moved due to technical requirements (such as flight simulators) or servers hosting applications critical to Air Force, DOD, or combatant command missions.

3.2.2.4. Closed – Data centers not identified as one of the three categories above must be projected to close no later than 2018. Applications hosted within these data centers must be migrated to a data center approved by SAF/CIO A6 as noted below.

3.2.3. Application Designations. Applications and/or systems that do not require base boundary transit for use are designated local and may reside in an IPN approved by SAF/CIO A6. All other applications and/or systems are designated enterprise and must be hosted in an enterprise data center approved by SAF/CIO A6 NLT 4th quarter of Fiscal Year 2018 (QTR4FY18). Exceptions may be granted by SAF/CIO A6 for those instances where migration to an enterprise location would introduce risk to mission or an approved business case analysis shows migration to be cost prohibited. Application owners must coordinate with appropriate organizations as directed in Air Force Guidance Memorandum 33-04, Common Computing Environment.

3.2.3.1. DISA Core Data Center/MilCloud (any app, system, or service).

3.2.3.2. Commercial Cloud (any app, system, or service) with a DoD Provisional Authorization for the corresponding data level.

3.2.3.3. IPNs approved by SAF/CIO A6 (base local apps only).

3.2.3.4. SPPNs approved by SAF/CIO A6 (SPPN specific apps only).

3.3. Obligation of Funds Related to Data Centers (10 USC §2223a, Data Servers and Centers). Obligations, regardless of appropriation, other required approvals, or other granted authorities to acquire servers and/or equipment related to data centers (items specified below) as defined above must be approved by SAF/CIO A6 prior to execution. Exemptions are outlined below; however, data centers exempted under 10 USC §2223a, Data Servers and Centers must still be documented within the DCIMS, including IT components of weapons systems.

3.3.1. Exemptions to 10 USC §2223a, Data Servers and Centers:

3.3.1.1. Items acquired using National Intelligence Program (NIP) funds. This does not include Military Intelligence Program fund.

3.3.1.2. Items acquired using High Performance Computing Modernization Program (HPCMP) funds.

3.3.1.3. Items within data centers exempted from FDDCI as described in **paragraph 3.2.1**.

3.3.2. Items Covered Under 10 USC §2223a, Data Servers and Centers. This guidance applies to obligations of any and all funds to: construct or modify existing data center buildings, facilities, or rooms; or acquire items in the categories listed below regardless of appropriation, requirement, and/or originator.

3.3.2.1. Servers of any type.

3.3.2.2. Server software of any type.

3.3.2.3. Virtual Suites.

3.3.2.4. Storage to include Storage Area Networks (SAN), Network Attached Storage (NAS), and Direct Attached Storage (DAS).

3.3.2.5. Racks.

3.3.2.6. Uninterruptable Power Supply (UPS).

3.3.2.7. Generators.

3.3.2.8. Routers, switches, etc. (unless deployed in a facility separate from a data center or servers such as a wiring closet).

3.3.2.9. Cooling systems and environmental monitoring capabilities.

3.3.2.10. Backup capabilities, regardless of medium.

3.3.2.11. End user devices (e.g., desktops, laptops, tablets, mobile devices), and associated software and services used within a data center.

3.3.2.12. Service, support, and maintenance contracts (e.g., warranty support, preventive, routine, and emergency maintenance) for existing data center capabilities.

3.4. Data Servers and Centers Submission Preparation. Requests for obligation authority under 10 USC §2223a, Data Servers and Centers, must support a data center having an approved record in the DCIMS with a valid DOD identification number. All data centers must also have a corresponding and populated record in the Enterprise Information Technology Data Repository (EITDR). All requests for obligation authority and queries, to include requests for templates or support, must be submitted to the SAF/CIO A6 DCC team via the MAJCOM or FOA A6 to the AF Data Center Consolidation organizational mailbox: **usaf.pentagon.saf-cio-a6.mbx.a3c-a6c-afdcc-workflow@mail.mil.**

3.5. Data Servers and Centers Submission Process. Organizations must submit a spend plan for each data center maintained in DCIMS NLT 31 July of each year. Data centers in DCIMS without an approved spend plan on file with SAF/CIO A6 will be considered noncompliant. Spend plans must detail individual acquisitions for items listed in **paragraph 3.3.2** planned for the upcoming year and provide the information listed below in **paragraphs 3.5.1-3.5.7**. Organizations requiring acquisition of items not detailed on approved spend plans must submit an out of cycle request for approval to include the items listed below in **paragraphs 3.5.1-3.5.7**. Spend plans will be approved annually by SAF/CIO A6 to satisfy requirements under the purview of 10 USC §2223a:

3.5.1. Obligation Detail Matrix (format provided by SAF/CIO A6 DCC team).

3.5.2. Brief description for each acquisition.

3.5.3. A description of how each acquisition supports consolidation of infrastructure (FDCCI) and the JIE.

3.5.4. Individual purchase request or spreadsheet that shows item, quantity, and unit cost for each acquisition.

3.5.5. An approval memo signed by the wing commander, MAJCOM A6, PMO, or PEO and the approver/signer must be O6/GS-15 or higher. Approval memos must also certify that no capability exists within the base, MAJCOM, or program to satisfy the approved requirement.

3.5.6. All spend plans against a data center with an end state of "Closed" must be accompanied by an approved POAM, which clearly depicts closure before end of FY18. Moreover, the acquisitions for these data centers must clearly depict actions to realize closure.

3.5.7. A description of efficiencies realized including current and project savings in dollars or personnel, reduction in required floors space, or reduction in energy usage.

3.6. Approval Process and Timeline. The SAF/CIO A6 goal for completing review and granting approval or disapproval is 10 working days; however, this can be affected due to unforeseen circumstances. The "10 day clock" starts when all required inputs have been received and validated from the requestor. An approval code assigned by SAF/CIOA6 is required prior to execution of contracts or obligation of any and all funds for each item relating to those described in **paragraph 3.3.2**. Approval codes and associated items will be listed on the Obligation Detail Matrix attached to the SAF/CIO A6 approved spend plan and sent to the requestor.

3.6.1. Out of cycle approval codes may be obtained by sending an electronic message to the AF DCC Team at <u>usaf.pentagon.saf-cio-a6.mbx.a3c-a6c-afdcc-workflow@mail.mil.</u> Requests received prior to 1600 EST will generally be approved the same day with approval codes returned to the requestor. Requestors must present the validation e-mail provided by SAF/CIO A6 personnel via the "USAF Pentagon SAF-CIO A6 Mailbox A3C-A6C AFDCC Workflow" electronic mailbox along with the out of cycle approval code for funds to be obligated by a contracting officer. A SAF/CIO A6 approval memorandum and attached Obligation Detail Matrix must be provided for all obligations relating to items in **paragraph 3.3.2**, regardless of approval code disposition.

3.7. Requestor Reporting Requirements.   All changes to data center configurations (e.g. shutting down a data center) must be reported within 30 days of the event occurring. Actual obligation amounts must be reported within 30 days of the event occurring for each item on the Obligation Detail Matrix attached to approved spend plans. Failure to comply with these instructions or instructions issued in approval memoranda results in noncompliance for the data center.

WILLIAM T. LORD, Lt Gen, USAF
Chief of Warfighting Integration and Chief
Information Officer

Attachment 1

GLOSSARY OF REFERENCES AND SUPPORTING INFORMATION

References

AFI 25-201, *Intra-Service, Intra-Agency, and Inter-Agency Support Agreements Procedures*, 18 October 2013

AFI 25-201, *Supports Agreements Procedures*, 1 May 2005

AFI 33-134, *Mobile Satellite Services Management*, 10 February 2005

AFI 33-360, *Publications and Forms Management*, 18 May 2006

AFI 33-360, *Publications and Forms Management*, 25 September 2013

AFI 33-590, *Radio Management*, 8 April 2013

AFI 36-2619, *Military Personnel Appropriation (MPA) Man-Day Program*, 22 July 1994

AFI 38-101, *Air Force Organization*, 16 March 2011AFI 63-101, *Acquisition and Sustainment Life Cycle Management*, 17 April 2009

AFI 63-101, *Integrated Life Cycle Management*, 7 March 2013

10 U.S.C. §2223a, Data Servers and Centers

AFMAN 23-110, *USAF Supply Manual*, 1 April 2009

AFMAN 33-116, *Long-Haul Communications Management*, 16 May 2013

AFMAN 33-152, *User Responsibilities and Guidance for Information Systems*, 1 June 2012

AFMAN 33-153, *Information Technology (IT) Asset Management (ITAM)*, 19 March 2014

AFMAN 33-363, *Management of Records*, 1 March 2008

AFI 63-131, *Modification Management*, 19 March 2013

AFPD 16-5, *Planning, Programming, Budgeting, and Execution Process*, 27 September 2010

AFPD 33-1, *Cyberspace Support*, 9 August 2012

AFPD 33-1, *Information Resources Management*, 27 June 2006

AFPD 33-3, *Information Management*, 28 March 2006

AFPD 33-3, *Information Management*, 8 September 2011

DoD CIO Memo, *Approvals/Waivers for Obligation of Funds for Data Servers and Centers*, 26 Jun 2012

DoD CIO Memo, *Approvals/Waivers for Obligation of Funds for Data Servers and Centers*, 9 May 2013

DoD CIO Memo, *Exemption for Obligation of funds for data servers and data centers related to the High Performance Computing Modernization Program*, 25 January 2013

MPTO 00-33A-1001 *General Communications Activities Management Procedures and Practice Requirements*, 31 March 2010

MPTO 00-33A-1001 *General Cyberspace Support Activities Management Procedures and Practice Requirements*, 1 May 2014

MPTO 33D-2002-WA, *Cyberspace Engineering, Implementation, and Readiness Activities Management*, 30 May 2014

MPTO 00-33D-3003, *Managing the Cyberspace Infrastructure with the Cyberspace Infrastructure Planning System*, 30 December 2010

MPTO 00-33D-3004-WA, *Managing Cable and Antenna with the Cyberspace Infrastructure Planning System (CIPS) Visual Component (CVC)*, 16 July 2012

National Defense Authorization Act (NDAA) Fiscal Year 2012, § 2867, *Data Servers and Centers*, 31 Dec 2011

Public Law 112-81

T.O. 32-1-101, *Use and Care of Hand Tools and Measuring Tools*, 1 December 2004

Prescribed Forms

No forms are prescribed by this publication

Adopted Forms

AFTO Form 229, *Engineering Installation Assistance*

AFTO Form 747, *Cyberspace Infrastructure Systems Acceptance*

AFTO Form 330, *Base Blueprint Endorsement Checklist*

AF Form 673, *Air Force Publication/Form Action Request*

AF Form 847, *Recommendation for Change of Publication*

See MPTO 00-33A-1001, for other adopted forms.

Abbreviations and Acronyms

AF—Air Force (as used in forms)

AFC2IC—Air Force Command and Control Integration Center

AFCQCC—Air Force Communications Quality Control Check sheet

AFEMS-AIM—Air Force Equipment Management System-Asset Inventory Management

AFFOR—Air Force Forces

AFI—Air Force Instruction

AFIN—Air Force Information Networks

AFJQS—Air Force Job Qualification Standard

AFMAN—Air Force Manual

AFMC—Air Force Material Command

AFNIC—Air Force Network Integration Center

AFPD—Air Force Policy Directive

AFRC—Air Force Reserves Command

AFSC—Air Force Specialty Code

AFSPC—Air Force Space Command

AFTO—Air Force Technical Order

AIM—Asset Inventory Management

AIS—Automated Information System

ALC—Air Logistics Center

ANG—Air National Guard

BIN—Budget Identification Number

CDC—Core Data Center

CEIG—Cyberspace Engineering Installation Group

CFETP—Career Field Education and Training Plan

CFP—Communications Focal Point

CIO—Chief Information Officer

CIPS—Cyberspace Infrastructure Planning System

CITS—Combat Information Transfer Systems

CMDS—Communications Mission Data Set

CMO—Circuit Management Office

COTS—Commercial-off-the-shelf

CPCP—Corrosion Prevention and Control Program

CRA—Centralized Repair Activity

CS—Communications Squadron

CSC—Client Service Center

CSI—Cyberspace Systems Integrator

CSIR—Communications and Information Systems Installation Records

CST—Client Service Team

CVC—CIPS Visualization Component

DAS—Direct Attached Storage

DCIMS—Data Center Inventory Management System

DECC—Defense Enterprise Computing Center

DISN—Defense Information Systems Network

DNI—Director of National Intelligence

DOC—Designated Operational Capability

DOD—Department of Defense

DODIN—Department of Defense Information Networks

DRA—Defense Reporting Activity

DRU—Direct Reporting Unit

DSS—DISN Subscription Services

EI—Engineering and Installation (also E&I)

EIGS—Engineering and Installation Governance Structure

EITDR—Enterprise Information Technology Data Repository

ESD—Enterprise IT Service Desk

ETIMS—Enhanced Technical Information System

FAM—Functional Area Manager

FDDCI—Federal Data Center Consolidation Initiative

FOA—Field Operating Agency

GOTS—Government Off-The-Shelf

GSU—Geographically Separated Units

HPCMP—High Performance Computing Modernization Program

IAW—In Accordance With

IMDS—Integrated Maintenance Data System

IPN—Installation Processing Node

IT—Information Technology

ITAM—Information Technology Asset Management

JIE—Joint Information Environment

JTRS—Joint Tactical Radio System

LDL—Low Density Level

LSC—Logistics Service Center

LWC—Local Workcards

MAJCOM—Major Command

MOA—Memorandum of Agreement

MOC—Maintenance Operations Center

MOU—Memorandum of Understanding

MPA—Military Personnel Appropriation

MPTO—Methods and Procedures Technical Order

MSS—Mobile Satellite Services

MTO—Maintenance Tasking Order

NAF—Numbered Air Force

NAS—Network Attached Storage

NGB—National Guard Bureau

NIP—National Intelligence Program

NLT—No Later Than

NSS—National Security System

NTO—Network Tasking Order

O&M—Operations and Maintenance

OMB—Office of Manpower and Budget

OPR—Office of Primary Responsibility

PEC—Program Element Code

PMI—Preventative Maintenance Inspection

PMO—Program Management Office

POM—Program Objective Memorandum

QA—Quality Assurance

QAR—Quality Assurance Representative

RDS—Records Disposition Schedule

RSP—Readiness Spares Packages

SAF—Secretary of the Air Force

SAN—Storage Area Network

SAP—Special Access Program

SAV—Staff Assistance Visit

SCI—Sensitive Compartmented Information

SCT—Specialized Communications Team

SITREPS—Situational Reports

SLA—Service Level Agreement

SPPN—Special Purpose Processing Note (SPPN)

TACON—Tactical Control

TBA—Training Business Area

TCI—Time Change Item

TCNO—Time Compliance Network Order

TCTO—Time Compliance Technical Order

TFG—Total Force Group

TMS—Telephone Management System

T.O.—Technical Order

TODO—Technical Order Distribution Office

TRN—Turn-Around

UPS—Uninterruptable Power Supply

USAF—United States Air Force

WOMS—Work Order Management System

Terms

Air Force-Approved AIS—An Air Force-approved automated information system is any system that the Air Force maintains and operates at an enterprise level such as Cyberspace Infrastructure Planning System (CIPS), Integrated Maintenance Data System (IMDS), Training Business Area (TBA), Remedy, and Telephone Management System (TMS). MAJCOM-unique systems are not Air Force-level AISs.

Air Force Communications Special Instructions—AFCSIs provide a means to temporarily issue inspection and servicing requirements, operational performance checks, and special instructions related to standard communications equipment for which formal T.O. procedures are not yet published. They may also provide a means to issue optional or temporary modifications on communications equipment. They are only published for equipment that is applicable to more than one MAJCOM and until applicable T.O. can be developed.

Air Force-Global Information Grid (AF-GIG)—The Air Force-provisioned portion of the Global Information Grid (GIG) that the Air Force has primary responsibility for the procurement, operations, and defense. It provides global connectivity and services, in addition to C2 of that connectivity and those services that enable Air Force commanders to achieve information and decision superiority in support of Air Force mission objectives. The AF-GIG consists of fixed, mobile, and deployable facilities, and equipment, as well as processes, trained personnel and information.

Assets/Commodities—Refers to the list of communications categories that provide a communications capability: Distribution Systems, Data, Flight Support Systems, Long Haul Comm., Network Control Center, Premise Wiring, Public Address, Radio, Security, Video, and Voice Switching Systems. This includes equipment and infrastructure.

Cannibalization—Cannibalization is the removing of parts from one end item and placing the removed parts into another like item. This is done to restore systems/equipment quickly. The part is then ordered and installed into the item which the part was removed from to restore the first item.

Centralized Repair Activity (CRA)—Consolidates support and supply resources at designated locations to support dispersed equipment. It integrates support, supply and other logistics elements providing a cohesive support program that enhances logistics responsiveness and operational effectiveness while reducing costs (see AFMAN 23-110 Volume 2, Part 2, Chapter 21, Section 21N).

Certified Personnel—Certified personnel are qualified personnel who have completed hands-on performance training designed to qualify an airman in a specific position (duty position or skill-level), however they have been evaluated by an outside source (e.g., QA, Stan/Eval, Cisco, Microsoft, etc). In the CFETP, the task certifier block is used to document third party certifications if required by your Air Force Career Field Manager (AFCFM). Not all tasks require certification on the CFETP however once that specific task has been certified by an outside source, it can reflect that certification. Also to certify ATCALS equipment and systems, the qualified personnel needs to be certified on the equipment or systems being ATCALS certified.

Client Service Center (CSC)—The Client Service Center (CSC) is the work center that will perform the following functions Communications Focal Point, Voice/Video/Data/Personnel Wireless Communications System Appliances, Account Management, and Asset Management. These functions are responsible issuing and tracking communications systems/equipment.

Commercial-Off-The-Shelf (COTS)—COTS systems or equipment are products/items designed and manufactured for commercial use, purchased, and used "as-is" by the military.

Cyberspace—Defined in JP 1-02 as "A global domain within the information environment consisting of the interdependent network of information technology infrastructures, including the internet, telecommunications networks, computer systems, and embedded processors and controllers." Air Force considers cyberspace to be a physical domain and therefore subject to all physical laws of nature. In a physical sense, the Air Force considers cyberspace to include things such as the internet (Global Information Grid or GIG), telecommunications networks (combat communications, satellite communications), computer systems, network operations and command and control [e.g., Air Force Network Operations Center, Integrated Network Operations Security Centers (I-NOSC)], and embedded processors and controllers.

Cyberspace Infrastructure Requirement—Add a new capability in the form of a new system, asset, or a change to the network/cyberspace infrastructure configuration that affects the Communications Mission Data Set (CMDS).

Cyberspace support activity—Any actions taken to restore communications systems/equipment to operational status, to perform preventive maintenance inspections (PMI) on communications systems/equipment, and/or component, or to install or remove communications systems/equipment.

Communications Focal Point (CFP)—CFP is the consolidation of help desk, telephone trouble tickets and Maintenance Operations Center. This function tracks all communications systems/equipment and/or component outages and resides with the Client Service Center (CSC) work center.

Communications systems/equipment—Any item maintained, restored, installed or removed by cyberspace personnel to include circuits. "Communications systems" are defined as: transmission, switching, processing, systems-control, and network management systems, as well as equipment, software, and facilities, fixed and deployable, that supports a mission area. Examples include: base telephone switches, cable plants, cable television, Automated Message Handling System (AMHS), Defense Message System (DMS), antennas, land mobile radio systems and cryptographic systems. The Air Force-provisioned portion of the Global Information Grid (GIG) that the Air Force has primary responsibility for the procurement, operations, and defense. It provides global connectivity and services, in addition to C2 of that connectivity and those services that enable Air Force commanders to achieve information and decision superiority in support of Air Force mission objectives. The AF-GIG consists of fixed, mobile, and deployable facilities, and equipment, as well as processes, trained personnel and information. This document implements DoD Directive (DoDD) 8100.1, *Global Information Grid (GIG) Overarching Policy,* and defines Air Force roles and responsibilities for protecting and maintaining the AF-GIG; and also encompasses terrestrial, space and airborne networks [networks are defined as all wired and wireless information (data/voice/video) exchange systems - even if not Internet Protocol (IP)-based].

Cyberspace-C—Defined in JP 102 as "A global domain within the information environment consisting of the interdependent network of information technology infrastructures, including the internet, telecommunications networks, computer systems, and embedded processors and controllers." Air Force considers cyberspace to be a physical domain and therefore subject to all physical laws of nature. In a physical sense, the Air Force considers cyberspace to include things such as the internet (Global Information Grid or GIG), telecommunications networks (combat communications, satellite communications), computer systems, network operations and command and control [e.g., Air Force Network Operations Center, Integrated Network Operations Security Centers (I-NOSC)], and embedded processors and controllers.

Cyberspace Infrastructure—Refers to the equipment and network infrastructure to provide the internet, telecommunications network, network operations, command and control and embedded processors and controllers.

Engineering Installation—Program that provides engineering, implementation, restoral, removal and reconstitution of Air Force cyberspace infrastructure. The program focuses on the highest priority cyber infrastructure requirements impacting the Air Force.

Executive Agent—Indicates a delegation of authority by a superior to a subordinate to act on behalf of the superior. An agreement between equals does not create an executive agent. Designation as executive agent, in and of itself, confers no authority. The exact nature and scope of the authority delegated must be stated in the document designating the executive agent. An executive agent may be limited to providing only administration and support or coordinating common functions or it may be delegated authority, direction, and control over specified resources for specified purposes.

Flight Commander and Flight Chief—Any officer, enlisted or civilian member fulfilling those duties serving over the flight of personnel.

Global Information Grid (GIG)—The globally interconnected, end-to-end set of information capabilities, associated processes, and personnel for collecting, processing, storing, disseminating and managing information on demand to warfighters, policy makers, and support personnel. The GIG includes all owned and leased communications and computing systems and services, software (including applications), data, security services, and other associated services necessary to achieve Information Superiority. It also includes National Security Systems as defined in section 3542(b) (2) of Title 44 United States Code (U.S.C.). The GIG supports all DoD, National Security, and related Intelligence Community missions and functions (strategic, operational, tactical, and business), in war and in peace. The GIG provides capabilities from all operating locations (bases, posts, camps, stations, facilities, mobile platforms, and deployed sites). The GIG provides interfaces to coalition, allied, and non-DoD users and systems. It includes any system, equipment, software, or service that meets one or more of the following criteria: transmits information to, receives information from, routes information among, or interchanges information among other equipment, software, and services; provides retention, organization, visualization, information assurance, or disposition of data, information, and/or knowledge received from or transmitted to other equipment, software, and services; processes data or information for use by other equipment, software, or services. (10 U.S.C. 2513).

Government Off-The-Shelf (GOTS)—Equipment, systems, and/or products that are typically developed by the technical staff of the government agency for which it is created. It is sometimes developed by an external entity, but with funding and specification from the agency. Because agencies can directly control all aspects of GOTS products, these are generally preferred for government purposes.

Hands-on—Any activity involving active participation to include actual performing the task at hand.

Joint Tactical Radio System (JTRS)—A Defense Department-wide initiative to develop a family of revolutionary software-programmable tactical radios that will provide the warfighter with voice, data and video communications, as well as interoperability across the joint battle space. The JTRS radios envisioned by DoD, expected to begin coming on line in the 2011 or 2012 timeframe, are based on software development that enables one radio to handle various waveforms.

IT Lean Process—The Information Technology Lean (IT Lean) process is a tailored version of the DOD 5000 series acquisition process specifically designed for small IT programs, and applies to systems in acquisition or sustainment including upgrades or modernizations. See AFI 63-101 for use of IT Lean in conjunction with the Security, Interoperability, Supportability, Sustainability and Usability (SISSU) process using EITDR to manage the acquisition process. See AFI 33-210 for use of IT Lean in certification and accreditation, and for scope and limitations of the IT Lean process.

Local Commercial Services—Telecommunications Services provided by the local exchange carrier (LEC) within the local area transport access (LATA).

Low Density Level (LDL)—Low density parts which are positioned at a LSC based on the number of TRNs submitted. There are very few of these parts available and it is a first come, first serve basis request. LSC manages this process in coordination with the unit.

Lead Command—The MAJCOM, DRU, or FOA assigned as the Air Force user advocate.

Maintenance Tasking Order (MTO)—Used by the AFCYBER community to assign workload to a field technician.

Network Tasking Order (NTO)—Used to direct changes to the Air Force-Global Information Grid (AF-GIG).

Quality Assessments—An element in the Quality Assurance (QA) program. Its purpose is to provide assurances, through some type of evaluation, that the Quality System functions are effective. Quality Assessment activities can be categorized as either internal or external assessments, evaluations, audits, or certifications. The QA program may use technical, personnel, and managerial evaluations to fill these requirements.

Quality Assurance (QA)—Embodies a leadership philosophy that creates and inspires trust, teamwork, and a quest for continuous, measurable improvement throughout the working/production environment in the organization. It is the commander's tool for ensuring that a process, end item or service is of the type and quality to meet or exceed requirements for effective mission operations. It performs regular evaluations on unit personnel, equipment, and programs to ensure unit is adhering to the instructions and technical publications and properly maintaining system/equipment. QA program consists of three essential elements: Quality System, Quality Assessments, and Trend Analysis. These three elements create an environment supporting the key objective of continuous process improvement.

Quality Assurance Representative (QAR)—Appointed by the commander, complete required training, then assist the QA work center in the accomplishment of evaluations.

Qualified Personnel—Personnel who have completed hands-on performance training designed to qualify an airman in a specific position (duty position or skill-level). Qualifications training occur both during and after upgrade training to maintain up-to-date qualifications and are used to determine qualified personnel. This does not mean personnel are certified.

Situational Reports (SITREPS)—Reports generated by a command and control authority/function that advises leadership of a situation.

Specialized Communications Team (SCT)—Provides a specialized maintenance and training capability above those normally found in the O&M units. SCTs perform emergency restoral of failed or degraded facilities, systems, or equipment and provide follow-on training to prevent recurrence of the problem.

Support Activities—Any actions or processes (e.g., publication management, time change management) that assist personnel with supporting the communications systems/equipment. The activities minimize fraud waste and abuse and provide common practices among all cyberspace personnel no matter the duty location.

System Affiliate—A MAJCOM or agency designated by a negotiated formal agreement with the lead.

Systems/equipment—See Communications systems/equipment.

Time Change Item (TCI)—Scheduled actions that personnel perform to support a piece of equipment. They are listed in the technical publications and occur as deemed. For example: replacement of the oil after 3000 hours of operation.

Time Compliance Network Order (TCNO)—Generated by AFCYBER/Air Force Combat Communications Center (AFCCC) and direct a change to systems/equipment. Air Force level TCNOs are converted to TCTOs if required by the Program Management Office (i.e., Combat Information Transport System [CITS], etc.).

Time Compliance Technical Order (TCTO)—Directs a modification or change to a system or piece equipment and are published by the Program Management Office (PMO).

Tools—Any device used to restore, repair, change, modify, clean, etc. a piece of communications equipment. Tools can be physical items such as a screwdriver, pad, resistor, junction boxes, hammer, pre-made cabling, etc., as well as software items such as restoral disks, software imaging disks, drivers, program software, disk duplicator, etc. These items need to be stored and maintained according to MPTO 00-33A-1001, T.O. 32-1-101 and unit guidance/policy.

Cybersecurity Titles Published by 4th Watch Publishing Co.

NIST SP 500-288	Specification for WS-Biometric Devices (WS-BD)
NIST SP 500-291 V2	NIST Cloud Computing Standards Roadmap
NIST SP 500-292	NIST Cloud Computing Reference Architecture
NIST SP 500-293 V1 & V2	US Government Cloud Computing Technology Roadmap
NIST SP 500-293 V3	US Government Cloud Computing Technology Roadmap
NIST SP 500-299	NIST Cloud Computing Security Reference Architecture
NIST SP 500-304	Data Format for the Interchange of Fingerprint, Facial & Other Biometric Information
NIST SP 800-12 R1	An Introduction to Information Security
NIST SP 800-16 R1	A Role-Based Model for Federal Information Technology/Cybersecurity Training
NIST SP 800-18 R1	Developing Security Plans for Federal Information Systems
NIST SP 800-22 R1a	A Statistical Test Suite for Random and Pseudorandom Number Generators for Cryptographic Applications
NIST SP 800-30	Guide for Conducting Risk Assessments
NIST SP 800-31	Intrusion Detection Systems
NIST SP 800-32	Public Key Technology and the Federal PKI Infrastructure
NIST SP 800-34 R1	Contingency Planning Guide for Federal Information Systems
NIST SP 800-35	Guide to Information Technology Security Services
NIST SP 800-36	Guide to Selecting Information Technology Security Products
NIST SP 800-37 R2	Applying Risk Management Framework to Federal Information
NIST SP 800-38	Recommendation for Block Cipher Modes of Operation
NIST SP 800-38A Addendum	Block Cipher Modes of Operation: Three Variants of Ciphertext Stealing for CBC Mode
NIST SP 800-38B	Block Cipher Modes of Operation: The CMAC Mode for Authentication
NIST SP 800-38C	Block Cipher Modes of Operation: The CCM Mode for Authentication and Confidentiality
NIST SP 800-38D	Block Cipher Modes of Operation: Galois/Counter Mode (GCM) and GMAC
NIST SP 800-38E	Block Cipher Modes of Operation: The XTS-AES Mode for Confidentiality on Storage Devices
NIST SP 800-38F	Block Cipher Modes of Operation: Methods for Key Wrapping
NIST SP 800-38G	Block Cipher Modes of Operation: Methods for Format-Preserving Encryption
NIST SP 800-39	Managing Information Security Risk
NIST SP 800-40 R3	Guide to Enterprise Patch Management Technologies
NIST SP 800-41	Guidelines on Firewalls and Firewall Policy
NIST SP 800-44 V2	Guidelines on Securing Public Web Servers
NIST SP 800-45 V2	Guidelines on Electronic Mail Security
NIST SP 800-46 R2	Guide to Enterprise Telework, Remote Access, and Bring Your Own Device (BYOD) Security
NIST SP 800-47	Security Guide for Interconnecting Information Technology Systems
NIST SP 800-48	Guide to Securing Legacy IEEE 802.11 Wireless Networks
NIST SP 800-49	Federal S/MIME V3 Client Profile
NIST SP 800-50	Building an Information Technology Security Awareness and Training Program
NIST SP 800-52 R1	Guidelines for the Selection, Configuration, and Use of Transport Layer Security (TLS) Implementations
NIST SP 800-53 R5	Security and Privacy Controls for Information Systems and Organizations
NIST SP 800-53A R4	Assessing Security and Privacy Controls
NIST SP 800-54	Border Gateway Protocol Security
NIST SP 800-56A R3	Pair-Wise Key-Establishment Schemes Using Discrete Logarithm Cryptography
NIST SP 56B R 1	Recommendation for Pair-Wise Key-Establishment Schemes Using Integer Factorization Cryptography
NIST SP 800-56C R1	Recommendation for Key-Derivation Methods in Key-Establishment Schemes - Draft
NIST SP 800-57 R4	Recommendation for Key Management
NIST SP 800-58	Security Considerations for Voice Over IP Systems
NIST SP 800-60	Guide for Mapping Types of Information and Information Systems to Security Categories
NIST SP 800-61 R2	Computer Security Incident Handling Guide
NIST SP 800-63-3	Digital Identity Guidelines
NIST SP 800-63a	Digital Identity Guidelines - Enrollment and Identity Proofing
NIST SP 800-63b	Digital Identity Guidelines - Authentication and Lifecycle Management
NIST SP 800-63c	Digital Identity Guidelines- Federation and Assertions
NIST SP 800-64 R2	Security Considerations in the System Development Life Cycle
NIST SP 800-66	Implementing the Health Insurance Portability and Accountability Act (HIPAA) Security Rule
NIST SP 800-67 R2	Recommendation for Triple Data Encryption Algorithm (TDEA) Block Cipher - Draft
NIST SP 800-70 R4	National Checklist Program for IT Products
NIST SP 800-72	Guidelines on PDA Forensics
NIST SP 800-73-4	Interfaces for Personal Identity Verification
NIST SP 800-76-2	Biometric Specifications for Personal Identity Verification
NIST SP 800-77	Guide to IPsec VPNs
NIST SP 800-79-2	Authorization of Personal Identity Verification Card Issuers (PCI) and Derived PIV Credential Issuers (DPCI)
NIST SP 800-81-2	Secure Domain Name System (DNS) Deployment Guide
NIST SP 800-82 R2	Guide to Industrial Control Systems (ICS) Security
NIST SP 800-83	Guide to Malware Incident Prevention and Handling for Desktops and Laptops
NIST SP 800-84	Guide to Test, Training, and Exercise Programs for IT Plans and Capabilities
NIST SP 800-85A-4 PIV	Card Application and Middleware Interface Test Guidelines
NIST SP 800-85B-4 PIV	Data Model Test Guidelines - Draft
NIST SP 800-86	Guide to Integrating Forensic Techniques into Incident Response

NIST SP 800-88 R1 Guidelines for Media Sanitization
NIST SP 800-90A R1 Random Number Generation Using Deterministic Random Bit Generators
NIST SP 800-90B Recommendation for the Entropy Sources Used for Random Bit Generation
NIST SP 800-90C Recommendation for Random Bit Generator (RBG) Constructions - 2nd Draft
NIST SP 800-92 Guide to Computer Security Log Management
NIST SP 800-94 Guide to Intrusion Detection and Prevention Systems (IDPS)
NIST SP 800-95 Guide to Secure Web Services
NIST SP 800-97 Establishing Wireless Robust Security Networks: A Guide to IEEE 802.11i
NIST SP 800-98 Guidelines for Securing Radio Frequency Identification (RFID) Systems
NIST SP 800-101 R1 Guidelines on Mobile Device Forensics
NIST SP 800-107 R1 Recommendation for Applications Using Approved Hash Algorithms
NIST SP 800-111 Guide to Storage Encryption Technologies for End User Devices
NIST SP 800-113 Guide to SSL VPNs
NIST SP 800-114 R1 User's Guide to Telework and Bring Your Own Device (BYOD) Security
NIST SP 800-115 Technical Guide to Information Security Testing and Assessment
NIST SP 800-116 A Recommendation for the Use of PIV Credentials in PACS - Draft
NIST SP 800-119 Guidelines for the Secure Deployment of IPv6
NIST SP 800-120 Recommendation for EAP Methods Used in Wireless Network Access Authentication
NIST SP 800-121 R2 Guide to Bluetooth Security
NIST SP 800-122 Guide to Protecting the Confidentiality of Personally Identifiable Information
NIST SP 800-123 Guide to General Server Security
NIST SP 800-124 R1 Managing the Security of Mobile Devices in the Enterprise
NIST SP 800-125 (A & B) Secure Virtual Network Configuration for Virtual Machine (VM) Protection
NIST SP 800-126 R3 Technical Specification for the Security Content Automation Protocol (SCAP)
NIST SP 800-127 Guide to Securing WiMAX Wireless Communications
NIST SP 800-128 Guide for Security-Focused Configuration Management of Information Systems
NIST SP 800-130 A Framework for Designing Cryptographic Key Management Systems
NIST SP 800-131A R1 Transitions: Recommendation for Transitioning the Use of Cryptographic Algorithms and Key Lengths
NIST SP 800-133 Recommendation for Cryptographic Key Generation
NIST SP 800-137 Information Security Continuous Monitoring (ISCM)
NIST SP 800-142 Practical Combinatorial Testing
NIST SP 800-144 Guidelines on Security and Privacy in Public Cloud Computing
NIST SP 800-145 The NIST Definition of Cloud Computing
NIST SP 800-146 Cloud Computing Synopsis and Recommendations
NIST SP 800-147 BIOS Protection Guidelines & BIOS Integrity Measurement Guidelines
NIST SP 800-147B BIOS Protection Guidelines for Servers
NIST SP 800-150 Guide to Cyber Threat Information Sharing
NIST SP 800-152 A Profile for U.S. Federal Cryptographic Key Management Systems
NIST SP 800-153 Guidelines for Securing Wireless Local Area Networks (WLANs)
NIST SP 800-154 Guide to Data-Centric System Threat Modeling
NIST SP 800-155 BIOS Integrity Measurement Guidelines
NIST SP 800-156 Representation of PIV Chain-of-Trust for Import and Export
NIST SP 800-157 Guidelines for Derived Personal Identity Verification (PIV) Credentials
NIST SP 800-160 Systems Security Engineering
NIST SP 800-161 Supply Chain Risk Management Practices for Federal Information Systems and Organizations
NIST SP 800-162 Guide to Attribute Based Access Control (ABAC) Definition and Considerations
NIST SP 800-163 Vetting the Security of Mobile Applications
NIST SP 800-164 Guidelines on Hardware- Rooted Security in Mobile Devices Draft
NIST SP 800-166 Derived PIV Application and Data Model Test Guidelines
NIST SP 800-167 Guide to Application Whitelisting
NIST SP 800-171 R1 Protecting Controlled Unclassified Information in Nonfederal Systems
NIST SP 800-175 (A & B) Guideline for Using Cryptographic Standards in the Federal Government
NIST SP 800-177 R1 Trustworthy Email
NIST SP 800-178 Comparison of Attribute Based Access Control (ABAC) Standards for Data Service Applications
NIST SP 800-179 Guide to Securing Apple OS X 10.10 Systems for IT Professional
NIST SP 800-181 National Initiative for Cybersecurity Education (NICE) Cybersecurity Workforce Framework
NIST SP 800-183 Networks of 'Things'
NIST SP 800-184 Guide for Cybersecurity Event Recovery
NIST SP 800-187 Guide to LTE Security - Draft
NIST SP 800-188 De-Identifying Government Datasets - (2nd Draft)
NIST SP 800-190 Application Container Security Guide
NIST SP 800-191 The NIST Definition of Fog Computing
NIST SP 800-192 Verification and Test Methods for Access Control Policies/Models
NIST SP 800-193 Platform Firmware Resiliency Guidelines
NIST SP 1800-1 Securing Electronic Health Records on Mobile Devices
NIST SP 1800-2 Identity and Access Management for Electric Utilities 1800-2a & 1800-2b
NIST SP 1800-2 Identity and Access Management for Electric Utilities 1800-2c
NIST SP 1800-3 Attribute Based Access Control NIST 1800-3a & 3b
NIST SP 1800-3 Attribute Based Access Control NIST 1800-3c Chapters 1 - 6
NIST SP 1800-3 Attribute Based Access Control NIST1800-3c Chapters 7 - 10

NIST SP 1800-4a & 4b Mobile Device Security: Cloud and Hybrid Builds
NIST SP 1800-4c Mobile Device Security: Cloud and Hybrid Builds
NIST SP 1800-5 IT Asset Management: Financial Services
NIST SP 1800-6 Domain Name Systems-Based Electronic Mail Security
NIST SP 1800-7 Situational Awareness for Electric Utilities
NIST SP 1800-8 Securing Wireless Infusion Pumps
NIST SP 1800-9a & 9b Access Rights Management for the Financial Services Sector
NIST SP 1800-9c Access Rights Management for the Financial Services Sector - How To Guide
NIST SP 1800-11a & 11b Data Integrity Recovering from Ransomware and Other Destructive Events
NIST SP 1800-11c Data Integrity Recovering from Ransomware and Other Destructive Events - How To Guide
NIST SP 1800-12 Derived Personal Identity Verification (PIV) Credentials
NISTIR 7298 R2 Glossary of Key Information Security Terms
NISTIR 7316 Assessment of Access Control Systems
NISTIR 7497 Security Architecture Design Process for Health Information Exchanges (HIEs)
NISTIR 7511 R4 V1.2 Security Content Automation Protocol (SCAP) Version 1.2 Validation Program Test Requirements
NISTIR 7628 R1 Vol 1 Guidelines for Smart Grid Cybersecurity - Architecture, and High-Level Requirements
NISTIR 7628 R1 Vol 2 Guidelines for Smart Grid Cybersecurity - Privacy and the Smart Grid
NISTIR 7628 R1 Vol 3 Guidelines for Smart Grid Cybersecurity - Supportive Analyses and References
NISTIR 7756 CAESARS Framework Extension: An Enterprise Continuous Monitoring Technical Refer
NISTIR 7788 Security Risk Analysis of Enterprise Networks Using Probabilistic Attack Graphs
NISTIR 7823 Advanced Metering Infrastructure Smart Meter Upgradeability Test Framework
NISTIR 7874 Guidelines for Access Control System Evaluation Metrics
NISTIR 7904 Trusted Geolocation in the Cloud: Proof of Concept Implementation
NISTIR 7924 Reference Certificate Policy
NISTIR 7987 Policy Machine: Features, Architecture, and Specification
NISTIR 8006 NIST Cloud Computing Forensic Science Challenges
NISTIR 8011 Vol 1 Automation Support for Security Control Assessments
NISTIR 8011 Vol 2 Automation Support for Security Control Assessments
NISTIR 8040 Measuring the Usability and Security of Permuted Passwords on Mobile Platforms
NISTIR 8053 De-Identification of Personal Information
NISTIR 8054 NSTIC Pilots: Catalyzing the Identity Ecosystem
NISTIR 8055 Derived Personal Identity Verification (PIV) Credentials (DPC) Proof of Concept Research
NISTIR 8060 Guidelines for the Creation of Interoperable Software Identification (SWID) Tags
NISTIR 8062 Introduction to Privacy Engineering and Risk Management in Federal Systems
NISTIR 8074 Vol 1 & Vol 2 Strategic U.S. Government Engagement in International Standardization to Achieve U.S. Objectives for Cybersecurity
NISTIR 8080 Usability and Security Considerations for Public Safety Mobile Authentication
NISTIR 8089 An Industrial Control System Cybersecurity Performance Testbed
NISTIR 8112 Attribute Metadata - Draft
NISTIR 8135 Identifying and Categorizing Data Types for Public Safety Mobile Applications
NISTIR 8138 Vulnerability Description Ontology (VDO)
NISTIR 8144 Assessing Threats to Mobile Devices & Infrastructure
NISTIR 8151 Dramatically Reducing Software Vulnerabilities
NISTIR 8170 The Cybersecurity Framework
NISTIR 8176 Security Assurance Requirements for Linux Application Container Deployments
NISTIR 8179 Criticality Analysis Process Model
NISTIR 8183 Cybersecurity Framework Manufacturing Profile
NISTIR 8192 Enhancing Resilience of the Internet and Communications Ecosystem
Whitepaper Cybersecurity Framework Manufacturing Profile
Whitepaper NIST Framework for Improving Critical Infrastructure Cybersecurity
Whitepaper Challenging Security Requirements for US Government Cloud Computing Adoption
FIPS PUBS 140-2 Security Requirements for Cryptographic Modules
FIPS PUBS 140-2 Annex A Approved Security Functions
FIPS PUBS 140-2 Annex B Approved Protection Profiles
FIPS PUBS 140-2 Annex C Approved Random Number Generators
FIPS PUBS 140-2 Annex D Approved Key Establishment Techniques
FIPS PUBS 180-4 Secure Hash Standard (SHS)
FIPS PUBS 186-4 Digital Signature Standard (DSS)
FIPS PUBS 197 Advanced Encryption Standard (AES)
FIPS PUBS 198-1 The Keyed-Hash Message Authentication Code (HMAC)
FIPS PUBS 199 Standards for Security Categorization of Federal Information and Information Systems
FIPS PUBS 200 Minimum Security Requirements for Federal Information and Information Systems
FIPS PUBS 201-2 Personal Identity Verification (PIV) of Federal Employees and Contractors
FIPS PUBS 202 SHA-3 Standard: Permutation-Based Hash and Extendable-Output Functions

DHS Study DHS Study on Mobile Device Security

OMB A-130 / FISMA OMB A-130/Federal Information Security Modernization Act
GAO Federal Information System Controls Audit Manual

DoD	
UFC 3-430-11	Boiler Control Systems
UFC 4-010-06	Cybersecurity of Facility-Related Control Systems
FC 4-141-05N	Navy and Marine Corps Industrial Control Systems Monitoring Stations
MIL-HDBK-232A	RED/BLACK Engineering-Installation Guidelines
MIL-HDBK 1195	Radio Frequency Shielded Enclosures
TM 5-601	Supervisory Control and Data Acquisition (SCADA) Systems for C4ISR Facilities
ESTCP	Facility-Related Control Systems Cybersecurity Guideline
ESTCP	Facility-Related Control Systems Ver 4.0
DoD	Self-Assessing Security Vulnerabilities & Risks of Industrial Controls
DoD	Program Manager's Guidebook for Integrating the Cybersecurity Risk Management Framework (RMF) into the System Acquisition Lifecycle
DoD	Advanced Cyber Industrial Control System Tactics, Techniques, and Procedures (ACI TTP)
DoD 4140.1	Supply Chain Materiel Management Procedures
AFI 17-2NAS	Air Force Network Attack System (NAS) Volume 1, 2 & 3
AFI 10-1703	Air Force Cybercrew Volume 1, 2 & 3
AFI 17-2ACD	Air Force Cyberspace Defense (ACD) Volume 1, 2 & 3
AFI 17-2CDA	Air Force Cyberspace Defense Analysis (CDA) Volume 1, 2 & 3
AFPD 17-2	Cyberspace Operations

www.ingramcontent.com/pod-product-compliance
Lightning Source LLC
LaVergne TN
LVHW060144070326
832902LV00018B/2936